TRIALS AND TRIBULATIONS:

A COLLECTION OF POETRY

VOLUME III


DESTINY DAWN MCCANDLESS

(DEDICATED TO MY MOTHER, MY GUARDIAN ANGEL, MAY YOU REST IN PEACE.

10/26/62-11/27/16

## TURN THE PAGE

I FIND IT RATHER CRAZY THAT
AS I CLIMB MY WAY TO THE TOP

I LET HIM KNOCK ME DOWN AND
TAKE ALL THAT I HAD.

AS AN HONOR STUDENT, I AM
ABOUT TO COMPLETE MY
BACHELOR'S DEGREE.

THAT, ALONE, MAKES ME HAPPY
YET STILL SAD.

ALONE I WILL HAVE TO WALK
THE STAGE,

BECAUSE THE MAN THAT I
THOUGHT WAS HERE FOREVER

HAS NOW BECOME ONLY
HISTORY.

HE ROBBED ME BLIND RIGHT IN
FRONT OF MY FACE.

HE WAS SCREWING AROUND
WITH ALL OF THE WHORES IN
TOWN

HE SUPPOSEDLY CARED BUT
THAT QUICKLY WAS ERASED.

IT KNOCKED THE WIND RIGHT
OUT OF ME.

I DID NOT EXPECT FOR HIM TO
DO ME WRONG.

THEN HE TOOK MY MONEY, SOLD
MY TRUCK AND CLEARED OUT
ALL THAT WE HAD BUILT
TOGETHER SOLID AND STRONG.

COME TO FIND OUT THAT I
WASN'T ANYONE SPECIAL AT ALL
AND HE WAS ROBBING ME AS HE
HELD ME TIGHT

HE SOLD MY TRUCK AND RAN
OFF TO SCREW HER,

AND HE EVEN LEFT HIS
CHILDREN WITH ME THAT NIGHT.

I FELT AS IF I WOULD RATHER
DIE THAN LIVE,

AND I HARMED MYSELF TO EASE
THE PAIN.

WHILE HIS WHOLE FAMILY
TRASHED ME, HARRASSED ME,
AND THREATENED TO BREAK
MY BACK AGAIN,

WHILE AT THE SAME TIME
SAYING THAT I WAS ONLY
PSYCHOTIC AND COMPLETELY
INSANE.

I WAS HEAD OVER HEELS IN
LOVE WITH HIM

I TOOK CARE OF HIS KIDS LIKE
THERE WERE MINE.

BUT WHILE I WAS TAKING CARE
OF THEM,

HE RAN AROUND, BEING A
WHORE, ON THE GRIND.

FOR SOMEONE WHO PRETENDED
TO CARE ABOUT ME

I HAD NO FOOD, NO RIDE, NOR A
HOME FOR MY KIDS.

NO CIGARETTES, NO HYGIENE, HE
EVEN KEPT MY PHONE.

I WAS LEFT LIKE TRASH ON THE
SIDE OF THE ROAD

HE TOSSED ME JUST THE SAME
THE WAY THAT HE DID.

I THINK THAT IT IS LUDACRIS
HOW IN DEPTH HE WENT WITH
HIS LITTLE CHARADE

AND ALL I HAD BUILT UP
MATERIALLY

WAS THE FINAL PRICE THAT HE
MADE ME PAY.

I WENT MANIC AND ACTED LIKE
A FOOL

WELL A FOOK IS WHAT I WAS,
YOU SEE.

BECAUSE I WAS SO NAÏVE TO PUT
ALL OF MY TRUST IN HIM,

NOT SEEING WHAT HE WAS
ACTUALLY TRYING TO DO TO ME.

NOW, ALL THAT IS LEFT FOR ME
TO DO IS TAPE TOGETHER WHAT
REMAINS OF MY HEART,

AND FINISH THE LAST TWO
CLASSES THAT I HAVE LEFT,

WHILE I BUILD BACK UP FROM
ROCK BOTTOM A NEW START.

HE IS ALL THAT I EVER THINK
ABOUT.

PATHETIC, AFTER ALL OF THIS,

I ALREADY KNOW.

BUT HE WAS MY WORLD, MY
EVERYTHING

THAT I EVER LOVED MORE
THAN SIN, YA KNOW?

EVERYTHING HAS LEFT ME
FEELING SO LOST AND EMPTY,

ONLY A SHELL, I FEEL CONFUSED
ON WHO I AM  OR WHAT I AM
WORTH AT ALL, REALLY.

IF A MAN CAN PRETEND AND
NOT GIVE A DAMN IF I AM OKAY

THEN WORTHLESS AND NOTHING
TO ANYONE IS SURELY WHAT I
MUST BE.

IGNORANT AND OBLIVIOUS, I
FELL INTO A MANIC EPISODE

AND I CUT ON MYSELF ONCE
AGAIN.

IVE GOT SCARS DOWN MY ARM
AND ACROSS BOTH THIGHS

WHERE ALL I WANTED IS FOR
THE PAIN AND HURT INSIDE OF
ME TO END.

DAMN IT, WHY DO I FEEL AS IF I
HAVE TO HAVE A MAN IN MY
LIFE?

AND I ALWAYS FALL HEAD OVER
HEELS IN LOVE WITH WHOEVER
SAYS THAT THAY LOVE ME.

WHY DO I FEEL AS IF I NEED VALIDATION TO BE WORTH A FUCK?

WHEN THEY WEREN'T WORTH A DAMN TO BEGIN WITH,

AND I ONLY MADE THEM OUT TO BE.

HE NEVER WANTED TO MARRY ME LIKE HE SAID

AND HE DIDN'T WANT THE FAMILY ALTHOUGH HE TRIED TO PRETEND AS IF WE WERE ONE.

HE WALKED OFF AND NEVER LOOKED BACK,

WE WERE OVER, FINISHED, WE WERE HONESTLY DONE.

WAS I REALLY HAPPY LIKE I HAD CONVINCED MYSELF?

OR WAS IT A FANTASY THAT I
LIVED OUT WHILE I STAYED
DRUNK TO HIDE THE MISERY
AND THE PAIN?

MAYBE SUBCONSCIOUSLY I DID
KNOW THE TRUTH,

BUT ADMITTING IT WOULD MEAN
THAT I HAD TO FACE IT.

THAT WOULD KILL WHAT LOVE
ACTUALLY REMAINED.

ACTS OF DESPERATION AND
WORDS OF ANGER FILLED WITH
RAGE,

ITS TIME TO MOVE ON AND
GROW ON MY OWN,

CLOSE OUT THIS CHAPTER IN MY
LIFE....

TURN THE PAGE.

## CRAZY

SOME DAYS IT IS FAR FROM EASY

JUST TO HOLD MYSELF
TOGETHER

THE ANXIETY AND DEPRESSION
COME AND GO

REMINDING ME OF THE
UNDECIDED TEXAS WEATHER

I CAN FEEL MYSELF GETTING
ANXIOUS AND THAT ONLY MAKES
IT WORSE

I WANT TO MAKE EVERYONE
HAPPY AND NOT FRUSTRATED.

THIS ROLLER COASTER IS NOT A
BLESSING.

IT'S A CURSE.

IM NOT SURE WHEN IT ALL

REALLY STARTED TO BECOME
MORE MANIC.

THINKING BACK TO MY EARLY
TWENTIES

I REMEMBER NOT BEING ABLE
TO CONTROL THE PANIC.

SCARED OF LOSING A LOVER OR
FOR A RELATIONSHIP TO NOT
END.

ID PANIC AND START CRYING
HYSTERICALLY.

THAT IS HOW IT ALL WOULD
BEGIN.

ANGER FOLLOWED BY SADNESS.

AGAIN, ANGER FOLLOWED BY
FEAR

I START FUMBLING AROUND AND
MY ACTIONS AND WORDS

QUICKLY CHANGE TO THE POINT
WHERE IM NOT CLEAR.

I SEE HOW IM ACTING AND I
HEAR THE WORDS THAT I SPEAK

BUT NINETY TO NOTHING I GET
VIOLENT AND IN HYSTERIA,

IT CAN SOMETIMES LAST UP FOR
AT LEAST A WEEK.

BUT WHEN I MELLOW BACK
DOWN,

I AM EXHAUSTED PHYSICALLY
AND MENTALLY.

SO DEPRESSION CREEPS UP AND
THE MANIC BEHAVIOR'S
CONSEQUENCES ARE THEN WHAT
I START TO SEE.

BY THEN I AM USUALLY ALONE
ONCE AGAIN

REALITY HAS HIT ME AND MY
LIFE I WOULD RATHER JUST END.

MY MIND DWELLS ON DYING BUT
NOT WANTIDNG TO DIE, JUST AS
WELL...

WELCOME TO MY MISERY...

WELCOME TO MY HELL...

CALL ME CRAZY OR PSYCHOTIC

CALL ME NUTS OR WHATEVER
YOU WOULD LIKE TO CALL ME,

MY FRIEND.

BUT DO NOT EVER GET IT
TWISTED THAT I AM THROWED
OFF

AND MIGHT BE SHOOTING DOPE
AGAIN...

I REMEMBER MY CHILDRENS
FATHER FOAMING FROM THE
SIDES OF HIS LIPS

BEATING HIMSELF PHYSICALLY,

UNABLE TO GET A GRIP

WELL, THAT IS WHERE I HAVE
EVOLVED TO MENTALLY

MY MIND IS NO LONGER VERY
STRONG

CAUSING DEPRESSION AND AN
EMPTINESS

LIKE THERE IS NOT ANY WHERE
THAT I REALLY EVER WILL
BELONG.

## BILLY REED

WASTED DAYS AND WASTED
NIGHTS

HOW IN THE HELL DID LIFE SEEM
TO BE SO HAPPY?

CONSTANT GET DRUNK AND
THEN FOLLOWED BY LETS FIGHT

YOU WARNED ME ABOUT HER
THE VERY FIRST WEEK

BUT YOU ASKED TO COME BACK

THAT WAS MY SNEEK PEEK

FOURTEEN HUNDRED DOLLARS
IN YOUR ACCOUNT

SIXTEEN HUNDRED ON OUR
HOME

NINETY EIGHT CENTS FOR A PAIR
OF FLIP FLOPS FROM YOU
THOUGH

AND I FELT NEEDY AND
ASHAMED FOR ASKING,

AND I SHOULD HAVE BOUGHT MY
OWN.

YOU ARE ONE SHADY MOTHER
FUCKER

BUT IT IS WHAT IT IS

I LAY HERE SMILING BECAUSE
SOON YOU WILL ALSO

COMME TO FIND OUT THAT I GO
TO WAR WHEN YOU GET ME
PISSED.

## HERE WE GO AGAIN

SHE SWORE TO ALL OF THOSE
WHO LOVE HER

THAT ONCE SHE WAS CLEAN,
THERE WAS NOT EVER GOING TO
BE A TIME WHERE SHE FALLS
BACK DOWN AGAIN.

YEARS OF SOBRIETY, SHE WAS
WINNING..

UNTIL SHE WAS ROBBED OF HER
BELONGINGS, HER HOME, HER
TRUCK, AND LEFT ALONE IN THE
END.

HEAD OVER HEELS IN LOVE,

SHE ACTUALLY LET HIM TAKE
THE LEAD

SHE HAS ALWAYS BEEN THE ONE
IN CONTROL,

AND NOW SHE IS POWERLESS,
ALONE, AS HER HEART BLEEDS.

IT WAS ALL A BIG HUSTLE,

A GAME OR A SCAM YOU
BASICALLY CAN SAY.

IN AWE, SHE FELT HER CHEST
GROW HEAVY AND GOT DIZZY,

TAKEN FOR EVERYTHING AND
TAKEN FOR GRANTED,

AND SHE ALLOWED IT TO GET
THIS WAY.

IM NOT SURE WHAT HURT HER
THE WORSE,

WAS IT LOSING EVERYTHING SHE
OWNED

OR WAS IT FROM HIM LEAVING
AND NEVER THINKING TWICE?

SHE CATERED TO HIM HAND AND FOOT, AND GAVE HIM EVERYTHING SHE HAD.

HE CHEATED AND ROBBED HER AND IT COST HER

HER SANITY... ID SAY THAT WAS A PRETTY BIG PRICE.

HUNDREDS OF STRANGERS ON SOCIAL MEDIA

CALLING HER TRASH, A WHORE, AND A PSYCHOTIC BITCH THAT NEEDED TO BE BEAT.

SHE CRIED AND SHE STRESSED AND SHE KEPT THROWING EVERYTHING UP EVERYTIME THAT SHE ATTEMPTED TO EAT.

THE FIRST WEEK SHE WOULD HAVE NIGHTMARES OF SEEING HERSELF COMMIT SUICIDE.

SHE WATCHED AS HER FEET
TWITCHED WHILE SHE WAS JUST
HANGING THERE,

AS HE SAW HER AND NEVER
EVEN CRIED.

SHE COULD NOT BARE THE PAIN
ANY LONGER.

SHE BEGAN TO CUT ON HERSELF
ONCE AGAIN TO "EASE THE
PAIN"

BUT NOW THERE ARE SCARS UP
HER ARMS AND LEGS,

AND THE PAIN AND HEARTACHE
INSIDE OF HER STILL REMAINED.

WHAT HAD SHE ALWAYS DONE
BEFORE IN THE PAST

WHEN SHE NEEDED TO FEEL
NUMB AND NOT CARE ABOUT
ANYTHING ANYMORE?

SHE SCORED SOME DOPE, AND SHE DIDN'T HESITATE TO RELAPSE.

SHE GOT HIGH.

FOR THE LAST FIFTEEN DAYS,

SHE HAS HARDLY EATEN OR CAME OUT OF HER ROOM, SHE HAS BEEN ON IT AND HARDLY CLOSED HER EYES.

SHE HAS STAYED HIGH EVER SINCE

KNOWING THAT SHE IS ABOUT TO FINSIH SCHOOL.

AND THAT THE LAST FIVE YEARS WERE FOR SOMETHNG MORE THAN THIS.

SHE LOOKS UP AT THE SKY WONDERING IF HER MOTHER IS ASHAMED OF HER,

DOES SHE UNDERSTAND, GOD
HER SHE TRULY MISSES.

IF ONLY HER MAMA COULD HOLD
HER RIGHT NOW

SHE WOULD SAY DESTINY DAWN,
DAMN IT,

I SAID THAT WE GOT THIS

STOP WITH ALL OF THE CRYING.

YOU CANT LET HIM SEE YOU
HURT.

YOU HAVE TO ACT LIKE IT
DOESN'T BOTHER YOU.

SIT BACK AND HE WILL SOON
GET HIS...

AND SHE WOULD WIPE HER EYES
AND TRUST THOSE WORDS

BECAUSE HER MAMA ALWAYS
TURNED OUT TO BE RIGHT

BUT ...YOU SEE... HER MAMA HAS WENT TO BE WITH GOD IN HEAVEN

AND SHE WAS LEFT TO CRY HERSELF TO SLEEP AT NIGHT IN TEARS

AND BEING ALONE HAS ALWAYS BEEN HER NUMBER ONE GREATEST AND WORST UNRESOLVED FEARS.

SHE DOESN'T WANT TO BE SEEN AS ONLY A DISAPPOINTMENT

SHE WANTS TO GROW AND SOAR TO THE TOP WITH PRIDE

BUT SHE HAS A LITTLE REMINDER IN THE BACK OF HER HEAD THAT SHE CANNOT SAY THAT SHES SORRY SINCE MAMA HAS DIED.

## HOW AM I SUPPOSED TO FEEL?

YOU BROKE MY HEART LIKE NO ONE HAS EVER BROKEN IT BEFORE.

I CRIED AND I DIDN'T WANT TO KEEP ON BEING ALIVE.

MY LOVE FOR YOU WAS LIKE NONE THAT I HAD EVER FELT BEFORE.

THE THOUGHT OF YOU GONE, I THOUGHT THAT I COULD NEVER SURVIVE.

YOU WERE MY WORLD, MY EVERYTHING.

I LOVED YOU MORE THAN SIN.

YOU HURT ME BAD AND THEN MOVED ON.

NOT LOOKING BACK,

YOU JUST FORGOT ME, LEAVING
ME WITH NOTHING IN THE END.

## CORY T

WELL HELLO THERE STRANGER

IT SURE HAS BEEN A WHILE.

ONE THING THAT I KNOW FOR
SURE MY FRIEND,

YOU HAVE ALWAYS BEEN ABLE
TO MAKE ME SMILE.

I DON'T RECALL EVER FUSSING
OR FIGHTING WITH YOU

AT ALL THROUGH ALL OF THE
YEARS THAT WE HAVE BEEN
FRIENDS.

THAT IS SHOCKING BECAUSE I
CANNOT RECALL ANY OTHER
FRIENDSHIP THAT I HAVENT HAD
SOME TYPE OF DRAMA IN.

I GIVE YOU A HARD TIME AND
PRETEND THAT I DO NOT

RECALL SOME MOMENTS OF OUR PAST.

I HAVE BLOCKED OUT A LOT OF THINGS,

BUT I BELIEVE MY MEMORIES WITH YOU WILL FOREVER LAST.

I AM GRATEFUL FOR YOU IN MY LIFE RIGHT NOW,

FRIENDS ARE FEW AND FAR BETWEEN.

WHEN I WAS WITH BILLY IT WAS ONLY HIS PEOPLE THAT WE HAD SEEN.

YOU LOSE CONTACT OF PEOPLE DUE TO DRUGS, JAIL, OR JUST THE YEARS.

I AM GRATEFUL THAT WE SOMEHOW STILL STAYED IN CONTACT.

HERE THESE LAST TWO WEEKS
IVE BEEN LEFT IN TEARS.

THANK YOU FOR THE TRIP TO
THE CASINO,

AND TRYING TO HELP LIKE YOU
ALWAYS DO.

YOU ARE AN INCREDIBLE MAN,
CORY.

FOREVER AND ALWAYS I LOVE
YOU.


## WEAK

I GUESS AS I GROW OLDER,

I AM BEGINNING TO LEARN
MORE ABOUT WHO I TRULY AM

AND THE TRUTH TO ME REALLY
DOES SEEM STRANGE.

IVE ALWAYS THOUGHT THAT I
WAS THE SAME OL' ME WITH
NOTHING DIFFERENT,

NO SIGNS OF CHANGE.

BUT AS I ASSESS MY PAST,
TRYING TO LEARN WHO I AM
TODAY,

I NOTIE SOME REALLY BIG
DIFFERENCES THAT HAVE MADE
AN EFFECT ON WHAT ALL I DO
AND SAY.

I USED TO BE SO LOUD AND
HARD SPOKEN,

ALL OF THE TIME, YOU SEE?

AND IVE DRAWN MYSELF UP
INTO MY SHELL,

I GUESS IS A GOOD WAY TO
EXPRESS WHAT IM TRYING TO
SAY.

OF SOLITUDE INSTEAD OF OPEN
AND CAREFREE,

FEELING AS IF I WAS GOING
CRAZY AND ASSUMING THAT
EVERYONNE SAW ME AS JUST
PLAIN INSANE

I SOFTENED MY TONE AND
BOTTLED IT UP WITHIN MYSELF

LOCKING THE CRAZY FEELING
AWAY IN MY BRAINL.

ONLY PEN AND PAPER WOULD
BE WORTHY TO HEAR MY
THOUGHTS THAT IVE SOLEMNLY
KEPT TO MYSELF

AND THAT IS WHERE I SHIVER
REALIZING THAT I WAS JUST
LIKE A CANCER.

I HAVE BEEN DESTROYING MY
HEALTH.

IVE LIVED IN A NUTSHELL TRYING TO PLEASE EVERYONE EXCEPT FOR ME.

AND I WAS MISERABLE, AND I FELT A FAILURE IS WHAT IVE BECOME FOR EVERYONE'S EYES TO SEE.

I NOW KEEP TELLING MYSELF,

"DESTINY, YOU ARE FAE FROM BEING WEAK."

AND I WILL ONE MORE BE HEADSTRONG AGAIN...

MY BACKBONE IS WHAT I SEEK!

## WHAT CAN I DO OR SAY?

I CAN SIT HERE AND PICK MY
BRAIN,

MAKING MYSELF CRAZY AS I
POSSIBLY CAN.

OR I CAN FORGIVE AND TRY TO
FORGET,

SO THAT I CAN MOVE FORWARD
WITH THIS MAN.

ITS JUST SO COMPLICATED WHEN
ALL I CAN THINK IS THAT I
WASN'T ENOUGH TO MAKE HIM
STOP

AND I WAS REPLACED IN A
BLINK

I QUESTION HOW LONG HE KNEW
HER AND HOW LONG THAT THEY
HAD BEEN HANGING OUT

BUT IF I AM TRYING TO JUST LET IT GO

THIS IS NOT HOW I NEED TO GO ABOUT

I AM TERRIFIED THAT WHEN I LEAVE HIS SIDE

THAT THE TWO OF THEM WILL HOOK UP OR CALL

AND I WONDER WHAT GREAT FRIEND OF OUR INTRODUCED HIM TO THE SLUT FIRST OF ALL.

I SCAN EVERY CALL AND MESSAGE THAT I DO AND THAT I DON'T SEE

IM TRYING TO LET IT GO AND FORGIVE MY SOULMATE

BUT IM REALLY DRIVING MYSELF CRAZY.

I KNOW IT IS STUPID AND
WITHOUT TRUST THERES
NOTHING AT ALL

BUT I TRUSTED HIM BEFORE AND
IT PUT ME IN A SPOT

WHERE I WAS IN A CORNER, MY
BACK AGAINST THE WALL.

SO WHAT IS IT THAT I NEED TO
DO?

I NEED MORE THAN JUST
HEARIING HIM SAY

THAT HE LOVES ME AND ONLY
ME

AND STOP THAT BEING MY
PRAYER EACH PASSING DAY.

## WHAT IS LEFT TO FEEL?

WELL, ONCE MORE HERE I SIT

THIS TIME I AM MUCH MORE
CONFUSED.

I FEEL AS IF I NEED TO BE
REPROGRAMMED,

BECAUSE I DON'T KNOW WHAT
TO DO.

IF I CRY, I AM BEING A DRAMA
QUEEN

IF I LAUGH I AM PLOTTING OR
SCHEMING

IF I SCREAM I AM ACTING CRAZY

YET I SIT HERE SILENTLY LIKE
THIS

I ONLY DRIVE MYSELF INSANE

ONLY PAIN FEAR AND ANGER
AND RAGE

IN ME EXISTS RIGHT NOW,

I SORTA WISH THAT I COULD
EXPLODE

I DON'T WANT TO FEEL LIKE THIS
ANYMORE

BUT I CANT PICTURE MY LIFE
WITHOUT HIM IN IT EITHER

I DON'T WANT TO EVEN TRY

I AM SO LOST AND FEEL ALONE

LIKE ITS ME AGAINST THE
WORLD..

OPEN YOUR EYES.

PLEASE REALIZE IM NOT CRAZY
BUT MORE SCARED OF MOVING
ON AND MY LIFE NO LONGER
SHARED WITH YOU

YOU ARE THE ONLY THING
OTHER THAN THE KIDS THAT

MAKES ME FEEL COMPLETE,
DAMN IT.

## WHEN FOREVER ENDS

WHAT DO YOU SAY WHEN YOUR
FOREVER HAS ENDED?

WHAT DO YOU DO WHEN AL
YOUR DREAMS GET WASHED
AWAY?

WHO DO YOU CRY TO WHEN YOU
NO LONGER HAVE YOUR BEST
FRIEND?

WHEN YOUR SOULMATE HAS
COMPLETELY JUST CAST YOU
AWAY?

HOW DO YOU LET GO WHEN FOR
SIX YEARS NOW YOU HAVE
CONSTANTLY FOUGHT TO JUST
HOLD ON?

HOW DO YOU COME TO REALIZE
THAT THE MAN YOU PROMISED
FOREVER'S LOVE FOR YOU IS
GONE?

WHERE DO YOU GO AND BE "AT
HOME"?

IF THE HOME YOU ARE
COMFORTABLE WITH YOU HAVE
TO LEAVE BEHIND?

HOW DO YOU FIND A NEW
BEGINNING WHEN YOU YOURSELF
FEEL LIKE YOU MAY BE TOO LOST
FOR ANYONE TO FIND?

## WINNING RACE

IN A WORLD WHERE IT SEEMS
ONE IS DESTINED TO LOSE

I SET OUT DETERMINED BUT YET
END SO CONFUSED

THE HARDER I TRY THE MORE
THAT I AM SLAPPED IN THE
FACE

I WANT TO GIVE UP BUT YET
YOUR LOVE CANNOT BE
REPLACED

SO AM I RUNNING A RACE
WHERE I KNOW THAT I CANNOT
WIN?

OR AM I HOLDING ON WITHOUT A
DOUBT KNOWING THE GOOD
TIMES WILL ONCE MORE
EVENTUALLY BEGIN?

## BEYOND A BLESSING

SOMETIMES LIFE APPEARS TO BE
WAY BEYOND A BLESSING

YET A MAJORITY OF THE TIME
LIFE IS A LIVING HELL

I MANAGE THINGS GOOD
THROUGHOUT THE DAY

GOING TO BED OR IN THE
EVENINGS IT SEEMS THAT THINGS
DO NOT GO QUITE AS WELL.

I KNOW THAT THIS TOO SHALL
PASS

AND IT WONT BOTHER ME AT
ALL IN THE DAYS AHEAD

I FIND PEACE AND SATISFACTION
IN THAT AFTER ALL OF THE
TEXTS THAT I HAVE NOW READ

NOW MY CONFUSION IS BUILT
AROUND ME

I THOUGHT THAT IT WAS THE
HAPPIEST THAT I HAVE EVER
BEEN

ALL HIS ACTIONS I FAILED TO SEE

SO HOW CAN IT BE EASY FOR ME
TO TRY TO MOVE ON

WHEN MY HAPPIEST WAS BASED
ON WHAT HE FOUND JOY IN AND
NOT ME AT ALL?

A WHOLE LOT OF EVALUATING
AND TRIAL AND ERROR TO
EVENTUALLY LEARN

I KNEW NOTHING ABOUT MYSELF
AT ALL.

NOW ALL OF THAT IS
CHANGINGAND I AM LEARNING
AS WELL TO GET BY

OTHERS OPINIONS NO LONGER
MATTER TO ME

I DIDN'T MATTER TO THEM
WHEN I WANTED TO DIE

ILL BE OKAY AND ITLL JUST BE A
LITTLE WHILE

THE REASON THAT I AM
REASSURED IS BECAUSE I CAN
FIND MORE REASONS NOW TO
JUST SMILE.

## BRANDON

SCROLLING THROUGH THE
INTERNET

DATING SITES ALL NEW TO ME

LOOKING FOR CODY'S PROFILE,

BUT YET YOU ARE INSTEAD
WHAT I SEE.

THREE WEEKS LATER WE HAVE
OUR FIRST FUSS

A MAJOR MISUNDERSTANDING
THE BOTH OF US YELLED AND
CUSSED

YOU AGREED TO FRIENDS WITH
BENEFITS

YET EVERY DAY YOU ASK ME TO
STAY

AND I FEEL WE MAKE LOVE
INSTEAD OF JUST FUCK

YOU ARE STEALING MY HEART
THIS WAY

HEAD OVER HEELS YET NOT
WHAT YOU WANT TO BE

I CANNOT ONLY BE FRIENDS TO
YOU

BECAUSE I HAVE FALLEN IN LOVE
WITH YOU,

YOU SEE...

## MORE THAN I CAN BARE

ONE EVENT RIGHT AFTER THE
OTHER

LIFE HAS SEEMED TO BECOME
MORE THAN WHAT I CAN BARE

I WENT THROUGH TREATMENT,
LOST MY MAMA TO CANCER,
CODY WENT TO JAIL AND AFTER
EIGHT MONTHS ON MY OWN HE
CAME BACK.

I GOT MARRIED, I MOVED INTO A
HOUSE, CODY RELAPSED AND
HIS ISSUES SEEMED TO JUST
CONTINUE TO STACK.

FIVE MONTHS AFTER THE
WEDDING RIGHT DOWN TO THE
ACTUAL DAY

I DID WHAT I THOUGHT THAT I'D
NEVER IN LIFE DO

AND DIVORCING MY SOULMATE
AND OTHER HALF IS THE PRICE
THAT I HAD TO PAY.

LORD, I NEEDED MY MOM MORE
THAN EVER,

AND MY FAMILY LIKED TO GOSSIP
BUT NEVER TRIED

TO CALL OR TO COME BY JUST
TO CHECK ON ME

TWELVE DAYS OF DEPRESSION....I
ALMOST DIED.

I HAD A BREAKDOWN, A MIDLIFE
CRISIS

SOME WOULD SEEM TO SAY

I PIERCED MY FACE AND SHAVED
MY HEAD AND I RAN TO
WHOMEVER DAY AFTER DAY

I MET BRANDON SHORTLY
AFTER,

IN THE MIDDLE OF THE STORM
AND PAIN I RAN AGAINST

I LATCHED ON CONVINCED THAT
I LOVED HIM

ALTHOUGH SEX IS THE MOST I
REALLY KNEW ABOUT HIM

HE WAS THE ONE THAT I SOON
CONVINCED

THREE MONTHS LATER HE
COULD NO LONGER BARE MY
CRAZY

I COULDN'T BARE TO BE ONLY A
PIECE OF ASS

HE SWORE THAT HE CARED
ABOUT ME

BUT IVE MADE UP MY MIND
THAT IT WILL NEVER LAST

HE WAS SO ARROGANT AND HE
WAS AN ASSHOLE

I WAS FRAGILE AND AND
BROKEN BEYOND WHAT I CAN
REPAIR

A TRAINWRECK NO DOUBTEDLY
IT WOULD BE ANOTHER PAIN

THAT I WOULD EVENTUALLY
HAVE TO BARE

PREMISCUOUS AND TAUNTING

NOTHING MATTERS TO ME
ANYMORE

FUCK GIVING MY HEART AND
SOUL TO ANOTHER

RANDOM SEX PREVENTS THE
PAIN OF BEING A WHORE.

## CRAZY AND CHAOTIC LIFE

LIFE HAS BEEN COMPLETELY
CRAZY

CHAOS AND DRAMA NEVER
SEEM TO END

IT GETS OLD AFTER A WHILE

NO WONDER THE REASON THAT I
HAVE NO FRIENDS

BUT NO MATTER THE STRUGGLE
AND NO MATTER HOW MUCH
CAUSES ME TO STRESS

TODAY I CAN STILL IDENTIFY ALL
OF THE MANY BLESSINGS IN THIS
HELACIOUS MESS.

PEOPLE ASK ME WHERE I FINND
MY MOTIVATION

I REPLY THAT WITH THE
STRUGGLE I FIND WHAT
MOTIVATES ME

REFUSING TO SIT ON IDLE AND
GO CRAZY

REFUSING TO LET SATAN WIN
THE BATTLE OVER ME

MEN USE ME FOR WHAT THEY
CAN GET

LINED UP TO TRY FOR A CHANCE
TO GET ME IN BED

BROKEN HEARTED AND
SHATTERED WITHIN MY SOUL

I JUST KEEP LOVING LIKE IVE
NEVER HURT INSTEAD

A BLEEDING HEART AND AN
UNTRUSTING HEAD,

A MIND FULL OF DOUBT,

EYES THAT SEE REAL, EARS
HEARING THE TRUTH BEHIND
WHAT ALL OF THE LIES SEEM TO
BE ABOUT.

MY MAMA ALWAYS TOLD ME
THAT WE GOT THIS

SHE MIGHT BE GONE BUT I STILL
FEEL THE SAME

WITH MY BABIES IN MY ARMS
AND GOD IN MY HEART, MY
MAMA WATCHING DOWN, AND
MCCANDLESS MY LAST NAME

I'LL OVERCOME, ILL KEEP MY
FAITH,

AND IN ALL OF THE BAD ILL FIND
SOMETHING GOOD

THE PAST IS THE PAST AND
FOREVER IT STAYS BEHIND ME

GODS GOT BLESSINGS AHEAD
FOR ME FOR THE FAITH IVE
WITHSTOOD

SO, THIS TOO SHALL PASS

TOMORROW IS A NEW DAY

GIVE IT ALL TO GOD AND GO TO
SLEEP

PRAY FOR OTHERS WHEN THEY
DO ME WRONG

LOVE OTHERS WITH ALL I HAVE
TO GIVE

KEEP FAITH THAT'S STRONG AND
DEEP

## <u>WHEN WILL IT BE ENOUGH?</u>

WHEN WILL IT EVENTUALLY BE
ENOUGH?

WHEN WILL OU SEE HOW MUCH
YOU ARE WORTH?

WHEN WILL YOU SEE THAT
THERES NO VALUE FOUND IN
THE MATERIAL THINGS ON
EARTH?

YOU ARE THE DAUGHTER OF A
KING

HIS LOVE ALONE CAN MOVE
MOUNTAINS AND CAN PART IN
HALF THE SEA

EACH ACT OF KINDNESS EACH
GOOD DEAD THAT I HAVE
SELFLESSLY DONE

HAS EARNED ME AJEWEL WITHIN
MY CROWN

STOP THINKING THAT ITS ALL DONE FOR NON.

WHEN YOU STOP LIVING LIFE TO FEEL SELF SATISFIED

YOU WILL UNDERSTAND HOW PRICELESS YOU TRULY ARE, NO DOUBT.

YOU WILL STOP SETTLING FOR NOTHING ANYMORE AND YOU WILL SEEK BETTER INSIDE AND OUT.

REMEMBER THAT MISERY LOVES COMPANY AND THAT SATAN IS TRYING TO STEAL

BUT HE IS JUST A LIAR AND A THIEF

GOD IS WITHIN YOU AND YOU ARE REAL

ALL OF YOUR EFFORT WILL SOON
PAY OFF

BLESSINGS ARE ABOUT TO FLOOD
YOUR DAYS.

KEEP YOUR FAITH AND YOUR
CHIN UP

GOD WILL REWARD YOUR
DEVOTIONAL PRAISE

WIPE YOUR EYES BABY GIRL AND
GO DRY YOUR ROSY FACE

THIS WORLD IS A MERE DESERT
IN COMPARISON TO OUR
FATHER'S GLORY AND GRACE.

ALL THE MEN WHO LEFT YOU
HURTING AND ALL THE FAMILY
THAT FAILED TO BE BY YOUR
SIDE WHEN YOU NEEDED THEM
THE MOST

ALL THE NEGATIVE THOUGHTS
AND POOR PERCEPTIONS OF
WHO YOU REALLY ARE

WILL BE TOSSED AS FAR TO THE
EAST AND WEST COASTS

LOOK INTO THE MIRROR AND
SEE THE BEAUTY THAT GOD HAS
MADE TO BE

HE DOESN'T MAKE MISTAKES, HE
HAS A PLAN WE ARE NOT
SUPPOSED TO UNDERSTAND

STAY ON PATH AND LOOK
STRAIGHT AHEAD DURING THE
STORM THAT YOU THINK WILL
BREAK YOU

REACH OUT AND TAKE GOD'
HAND

WHEN YOU ARE ONLY AIMING TO
PLEASE GOD AND FIND PEACE
LIVING WITHIN YOUR OWN SKIN

KNOW THAT GOD'S PURPOSE IS
LOVE, HIS GIFT IS GRACE,

AND HE ONLY WANTS TO HAVE A
RELATIONSHIP WITH YOU, MY
FRIEND.

GOD WILL HANDLE THOSE WHO
HURT YOU

HE NEVER WANTS TO SEE HIS
CHILDREN IN PAIN

LIVE ONLY TO MAKE GOD HAPPY
AND YOUR JOY WILL BE WHAT IT
IS THAT YOU SOON WILL GAIN.

THE TREASURES IN HEAVEN
THAT ARE WAITING

CANNOT BE COMPARED TO
ANYTHING THAT WASTES AWAY
BARE

TO RUN TO OUR FATHER THE
DAY WE HURT NO LONGER

WITH HIJM WHO ARE WE TO
FEAR?

## <u>WELL HELLO THERE, MAMA</u>

WELL HELLO THERE, MAMA

I SURE HAVE MISSED YOU...MORE
THAN I COULD HAVE EVER
POSSIBLY THOUGHT THAT I
WOULD.

I KNOW THAT HERE LATELY I LET
YOU COMPLETELY DOWN, BUT
AFTER ALL ON EARTH YOU HAD
WENT THROUGH,

I FEEL IF ANYONE COULD
UNDERSTAND THAT YOU COULD.

I TOOK FOR GRANTED YOUR
WORRY AND ALL OF YOUR
ADVICE

NOW THE WORRY, I TOO
UNDERSTAND

THE BROKEN HEART AND EMPTY
SHELL REMAINS THIS TIME

IT ISNT THE FOREVER THAT I
HAD PLANNED

IM GRATEFUL FOR THIS
STRUGGLE, IT HAS HELPED ME
FIND MY STRENGTH.

A BLESSING OR A LESSON JUST
THE SAME FOR ANY MAN

COMING TO UNDERSTAND YOUR
STRENGTH HAS LEFT ME
AMAZED AND IN AWWWE.

YOU PUSHED ON AND KEPT FACE
IN FRONT OF US KIDS,

YOU SHEDDING A TEAR WE VERY
RARELY ACTUALLY SAW

I PROMISE THAT ILL GET
THROUGH THIS STRUGGLE

SATAN WILL NOT WIN

THERE WILL SOON COME A DAY
WHERE I RUN TO YOU WITH OPEN
ARMS

RISKING THAT MOMENT ALONE IS
A SIN

PLEASE GUIDE ME ON MAMA

LEAD ME IN THE RIGHT WAY

ALONE I AM SCARED AND LOST
MY WAY OF DIRECTIONS

I FEEL SHATTERED AND SCARED,
SO TO SAY.

ILL BE HOME SOON, MAMA.

THIS WORLD IS A LIFETIME FOR
EACH OF YOUR SINGLE DAYS

SO AS I FIGHT ON WHAT FEELS TO
BE FOREVER TO GET THERE
BESIDE YOU

GOD'S WILL FOR ME IN MY HEAD
WILL STAY.

## <u>NO WHERE THE SAME</u>

TEN MONTHS AGO TOMORROW,

I WAS NO WHERE CLOSE TO THE
SAME ME

MY LIFE REVOLVED AROUND
CHAOS.

MY ONLY KNOWN EMOTION WAS
MISERY.

I STARTED MY NEXT JOURNEY
OVERWHELMED WITH FEAR

LOSING EVERY OUNCE OF SELF
ESTEEM AND HAPPINESS,

MY FUTURE WAS FAR BEYOND
ANYTHING THAT MIGHT SEEM
CLEAR.

AS SOON AS I STARTED LOVING
ME AGAIN

A WARMTH OVERWHELMED MY
HEART AND SOUL.

AND THEN THE DAY CAME TO
MEET CODY

AND THAT FEELING I HAVE
NEVER BEFORE EVER KNOWN

IVE NEVER BEFORE DEFINED
LOVE AS BEING WHAT I HAVE
FOR HIM AND FOR OUR LIFE

AND AT THIRTY THREE YEARS
OLD,

I CAN VISION THE POSSIBILITY OF
BEING SOMEONE'S WIFE

MY SOUL AND HEART NO
LONGER ACHE

MY EMOTIONS FEEL CRAZY TO
ME BECAUSE THEY ARE NO
LONGER RAGE.

NO LONGER AM I A VICTIM OR
SOMEONE'S PUPPET

I NO LONGER FEEL LIKE A RAT
INSIDE A CAGE

THESE LAST TEN MONTHS HAVE
FLOWN RIGHT BY AND I PRAY
THAT THE NEXT ARE THE SAME
WAY TOO

I WANT TO SMILE AND
APPRECIATE THE FEELINGS OF
MY FAMILY AND IN LOVE

AS LONG AS IT CAN HONESTLY
BE TRUE.

## PLAYING THE SAME GAME

THE ONLY REASONING THAT I
CAN MAKE IT OUT TO BE

IS THAT I AM CRAZY AND OUT OF
MY MIND SERIOUSLY

I LOVE YOU WITH ALL OF MY
HEART AND SOUL AND I TRUST
THAT YOU LOVE ME JUST AS
MUCH THE SAME

BUT WITH MY RECORD OF
RELATIONSHIPS IN MY PAST

THEY ALL HAVE ENDED WITH
THEM PLAYING THE SAME GAME

I SKITZ OUT WHEN YOU KEEP
YOUR PHONE ON SILENT

I QUESTION WHO AND WHERE
YOU ARE AT OR AROUND

ONLY BECAUSE I SIT HERE
ALONE IN MY HEAD ALL DAY.

THINKING THAT YOU ARE LIKE
EVERYONE BEFORE YOU ALONE
MAKES MY HEART SEEM TO
POUND.

## BOTH OF US

SHE BROKE YOUR HEART AND
HE WENT AND BROKE MINE

WE BOTH FELT LOST AND ALL
ALONE

THEN YOU LEFT ME BEHIND AND
NOT A DAY GOES BY

WHEN I DON'T FIND MYSELF
THINKING OF YOU

HIS MEMORY HAS NOW FADED
AND MY THOUGHTS ARE BRAND
NEW

YOU STILL ACHE FROM HER
MEMORY

YOU WONT LET GO OF THE PAST

ID PUT YOU BEFORE EVERYTHING

YOU WONT EVEN PUT ME UP
LAST

I SMILE THINKING ABOUT THE
NIGHTS WHEN YOU'D STAY

I CRAVED FOR YOU TO TOUCH ME
BUT YOU WOULDN'T GO THAT
WAY.

AFTER ALL THE BULLSHIT

IVE DROWN IN THROUGH
NINETEEN YEARS

IVE SEEN AND HEARD IT ALL

FOR THE LAST TEN MONTHS IVE
FELT NOTHING BUT
CONTENTMENT AND LOVE BUT
FOR SOME REASON IVE FELT
REALLY INSECURE AND DISTANT
FROM YOU

YOUR PHONE IS ALWAYS ON
SILENT

I DON'T KNOW WHY, ITS ALMOST
GOT ME PULLING BACK FROM
YOU

I GUESS IN FEAR IM GONNA GET
HURT ALL OVER AGAIN

IVE GOT A RING ON MY FINGER
BUT FEEL NO WHERE CLOSE TO
BEING ANYTHING OTHER THAN
YOUR GIRLFRIEND

I FEEL LEFT IN THE DARK SO ON
TO OF ME FEELING ALONE
NINETY PERCENT OF THE TIME,
MY BIPOLAR MIND ASSUMES ALL
SORTS OF SHIT FEELING MORE
DEPRESSED AND ALONE

ALL IVE EVER WANTED IN MY
ENTIRE LIFE IS TO FEEL LIKE
SOMEONE'S ONE AND ONLY

THE NEED TO BE NEEDED THE
WANT TO BE WANTED.

IT SOUNDS LIKE A LOT BUT ITS
REALLY NOT MUCH AT ALL

AND NOW AFTER THE LAST TEN
MONTHS,

I KNOW THAT I AM WORTH THAT.

IM JUST SAYING.

## I LOVE YOU, NICKIE

I LOVE YOU, BABY SISTER!

LOOK HOW MUCH OLDER YOU SEEM

OPEN AND TRUSTING

EACH DAY I FEEL CLOSER

YOU LISTEN TO ME, THE

OLDER YOU GET, YOU

UNDERSTAND ME MORE CLEARLY

MOW YOU ARE GETTING SO BEAUTIFUL

I KNOW YOU'LL HAVE ALL OF THE GUYS

CAUSE YOU ARE A KNOCK OUT

KICKING BUTT WITH THOSE EYES

I FEEL CLOSER TO YOU NOW.

EVERY SECRET THAT WE SHARE
REMEMBER THAT IM HERE FOR
YOU AND I WILL ALWAYS CARE.

## DAWN

I AM ALWAYS CAUSING TROUBLE

I DON'T LIKE IT ONE BIT

IT'S LIE IM IN A BUBBLE

THAT IS ALWAYS GETTING HIT

I WISH I WASN'T LIKE THAT

BUT WISHES DON'T COME TRUE

ITS LIKE I AM IN A HAT

THAT IS VERY SAD AND BLUE

I DON'T GET ATTENTION MUCH

BUT I DON'T GIVE A CARE

ITS LIKE MY DAD HIT A CLUTCH

WITH A LITTLE BITTY HAIR

ITS LIKE A WORLD WITHOUT ME

AND NO ONE GAVE A CARE

NO ONE IN THE WORLD COULD
SEE

AND NO ONE SEEMED TO DARE

I AM ALREADY WORN OUT

AND I AM ONLY NINE.

I ALWAYS WANT TO SHOUT

EVERYONE THINKS THAT I AM
BLIND.

## DEAR LORD,

I NEED YOUR COMFORT AND
YOUR GRACE

I AM BROKEN PAST WHAT FEELS
LIKE ANY POSSIBLE REPAIR

HE DID IT AGAIN AND TRIED TO
LIE ABOUT IT

AND THEN HE WALKED AWAY AS
IF HE NEVER LOVED OR CARED

DAYS OF DRUGS, JUST AS MANY
SINS, TEARS, AND TRUTHS THAT
ALL CAME TO LIGHT

HE WAS STILL GONE, I WAS STILL
LOST, AND I MASKED MY PAIN
WITH ANGER AND FRIGHT

CALLING OTHER WOMEN
CRUSHED MY SELF ESTEEM AND I
FELT LIKE I WAS WORTHLESS OF
BEING LOVED TRUE

SO I CALLED AND CUT OFF HIS
PHONE LINE

BECAUSE IT WAS THE ONLY WAY
TO LASH BACK AT HIM LIKE I
FELT THE NEED TO DO.

A WEEK LATER I AM STILL HERE
ALONE, A WAR WITH MY
CONSCIENCE AND WHAT WOULD
EASE THE ACHE

SCARED OF FAILING MY
CHILDREN AGAIN AND LOSING IT
ALL....MOSTLY YOU

EIGHT DAYS OF TEARS AND
HEART BREAK

ITS BEEN THREE DAYS WITHOUT
CONTACT

IM AT THE END OF ALL SANITY I
MIGHT HAVE HAD

I STARTED BEATING UP A GIRL
AND I COULD NOT STOP AND IT
ALL SEEMED TO END PRETTY
BAD

I GOT TO THE POINT WHERE THE
OBSESSION WITH WHAT HE WAS
DOING WAS GREATER THAN MY
RELATIONSHIP WITH GOD

YOU WERE A DRUG TO ME JUST
LIKE ANY OTHER

THAT TO IT I MAY FALL WEAK

I COULDN'T BRING YOU HOME
ANYMORE SO THE NUMBNESS I
THEN BEGAN TO SEEK

A NERVE PILL, A BEER, A
BOTTLE, A BOWL, SOMEONE'S
ARMS TO SHOW ME "LOVE"

RAGING FIGHTS, CIGARETTES AND BLARING MUSIC ISNT ENOUGH

WHAT IS IT THEN? WHAT CAN GET ME OVER THE PAIN THAT DWELLS INSIDE OF ME?

LET GO AND LET GOD... ANY BONDAGE WILL LET YOU SOON BE FREE.

ONCE MORE IVE GOT TO START OVER

LORD, GOD SAYS CHILD HAVE NO FEAR

DOUBT AND LACK OF SELF WORTH HOLD ME BACK

SATAN IS A LIAR, DON'T YOU HEAR???

FEELING LIKE ITS NOT REALLY SUPPOSED TO END SO FAST OR

AT ALL AND THAT ITS IN MY
CONTROL

IM REMINDED THAT MY WILL IS
LUDACRIS AND GOD'S WILL IS
HOW TO GO

ITS ALL ABOUT SURRENDER AND
HONESTY

WHEN GIVING MY LIFE BACK
OVER TO YOU

I KNOW ONLY YOU CAN RESTORE
MY PEACE AND JOY AND
HAPPINESS

NO MATTER THE CONSEQUENCES
I HAVE TO AGAIN TRUST IN YOU

PEOPLE SAY THAT YOU HAVE A
BETTER PLAN

THAT THERE IS A PURPOSE FOR
ALL OF MY PAIN

I TELL MYSELF IM TIRED OF
HURTING

THERES NO TRUTH BEHIND NO
PAIN NO GAIN.

TIME TO RID MY LIFE OF
DISTRACTIONS

IVE GOT TO FORGET YOU JUST AS
YOU HAVE ME

BUT YOU VOWED TO GOD FOR
BETTER OR WORSE AND I SAID
EVEN DEATH COULD NOT TEAR
US APART

I GUESS THAT THIS IS LIFE AND
EITHER A LESSON OR A
BLESSING THAT WENT BAD

EITHER WAY IT WAS ONCE VERY
SPECIAL

THE MOST REALEST LOVE THAT I
HAVE EVER HAD.

PLEASE DO NOT FORGET ME

PLEASE GET HELP WHILE I DO
THE SAME

WE DESTROYED ONE ANOTHER
WITH FINGERS AT EACH OTHER
POINTING BLAME

THE TEARS, NO TOUCH MY
JEALOUSY

MAYBE THIS WAS A REAL BIG
LESSON THAT GOD HAD FOR ME.

JUST KNOW THAT EVERY TIME
THAT I HEAR YOUR NAME MY
HEART WILL SKIP A BEAT

NO MESSAGES, NO CALLS, AND
NO COMEBACK...

I GIVE UP, I COLLAPSE TO YOUR
DEFEAT

GOD BACK IN CONTROL

JESUS TAKE THE WHEEL

PAIN MIGHT BE WHAT IT IS RIGHT
NOW

BUT PEACE IS WHAT I WILL SOON
ENOUGH AGAIN FEEL.

## WHEN THE GOING GETS TOUGH

SOME DAYS ARE MUCH EASIER
THAN OTHERS

SOME NIGHTS I CANNOT HELP
BUT TO JUST LIE THERE AWAKE

WHEN THE GOING GETS TOUGH IT
IS CLEAR NOW TO SEE

THAT YOU CAN TELL WHO AND
WHAT IS REAL FROM WHAT IS
FAKE.

ITS NOT WHAT I CAN OFFER YOU
AND ITS NOTHING TO DO WITH
WHAT YOU HAVE TO OFFER ME

ITS ABOUT WHO HOLDS YOUR
HAND WHEN YOU FEEL TOO
WEAK TO STAND

AND THOSE WHO DON'T JUST
ASK BUT MAKE SURE THAT YOU
ARE OKAY, YOU SEE..?

IF THEY JUST SIT AND WATCH
YOU STRUGGLE

THE REALITY IS THEY ARE NO
WHERE CLOSE TO BEING FAMILY
OR A FRIEND

THOSE TRUE SOULS WHO CARE
AND ARE COMPASSIONATE

KEEP US FROM BREAKING WHEN
WE BEGIN TO BEND.

### BRANDON STRAUB

BECAUSE THEY HAVE BOTH SEEN
HURT

REALLY BAD IN THEIR PAST

ACCEPTING A RELATIONSHIP
AGAIN IS

NOT ONLY TERRIFYING BUT
MIGHT NOT LAST

DRAWN TO HIM, SHE IS NERVOUS
AS HE'S THE

ONLY THING TO CROSS HER MIND

NEEDING TO FEEL HIM AGAINST
HER SKIN

SHE KNOWS HE'S THE FIRST OF
HIS KIND

SHE'S NEVER  MET AN HONEST
GUY

THAT HADNT LIVED THE LIFE
THAT SHE HAD

REALLY HEAD OVER HEELS IN
LOVE ALREADY

AND HE KEEPS SAYING TOO FAST
IS TOO BAD

UNVEILING HER HEART, HE SAT
THERE IN TEARS

BEAUTIFULLY INTIMATE AND
SOON A HEARTACHE IS WHAT
SHE NOW FEARS.

# HAPPY MOTHER'S DAY

HAVING A LOT TO DEAL WITH

AND THEN ALL OF MY STRESS

PUTS YOU IN A BIND

PLUS CLEANING ALL OF OUR
MESS

YOU ARE ONE HELL OF A
MOTHER


MORE THAN I CAN AMOUNT

OF COURSE ILL TRY TO BE

HAVING YOUR GUIDANCE WILL
COUNT

EVERY DAY I NEARLY CRY

REALIZING THAT MY BURDENS I

STACK YOUR WAY

DETERMINED TO MAKE

A DIFFERENCE

YOUR MY SUPPORT DAY AFTER
EACH DAY.

## ALONE WHILE HE RUNS ASTRAY

I WAS HAPPIER WITH LIFE THAN I
HAVE EVER BEFORE BEEN

I WENT FROM TRACK MARKS
AND BRUISES AND ABUSIVE
BOYFRIENDS

HE WAS COMPLETELY THE
OPPOSITE FROM ALL OF THE
MISERY IN MY PAST

ABOUT A YEAR INTO IT,

I WAS CERTAIN THAT FOREVER IS
HOW LONG WE WOULD LAST

THEN I DISCOVERED LIES WERE
HIS VICIOUS TRUTH

HAD I EVER TRULY KNOWN HIM?

I DON'T KNOW WHAT TO DO

SNEAKING AROUND AND
SHOOTING DOPE

SEXTING WITH WICHITA FALLS'
FINEST WHORES

OVER A HUNDRED MEET AND
FUCK SITES

AND THE HORNY EMAILS WERE
GALORE

HE PROMISED HE WOULD NEVER

DO STUPID SHIT LIKE THAT
AGAIN

LESS THAN THREE DAYS LATER
HE WAS SNAPPING DICK PICS TO
SEND TO HIS NEW FRIEND

HE NO LONGER TOUCHES ME

HE SHOVES ME OFF AS I TRY TO
MAKE LOVE

MY HEART IS COMPLETELY
SHATTERED

WHEN WILL I HAVE HAD
ENOUGH?

HE TELLS ME THAT HE LOVES ME

AND DOESN'T WANT TO LEAVE

BUT HIS EMAILS, PICS, AND
MESSAGES WITH THE LIES ARE
HARD TO BELIEVE

MY HEART IS NO LONGER
BREAKING FROM HIS ACTIONS
ANY MORE

MY HEART IS COMPLETELY
CRUSHED KNOWING ITS NOT
POSSIBLE TO GO BACK TO WHO
WE WERE BEFORE.

SOMETIMES I FEEL LIKE DYING,
JUST ENDING IT ONCE AND FOR
ALL

BUT I WOULD BE DEAD AND MY
KIDS ALONE, AND HIS LIFE
WOULDN'T BE AFFECTED AT ALL.

I GUESS I FEEL AS IF IM
DROWNING

MY CHEST IS HEAVY AND TIGHT

WHAT DID I DO IN LIFE TO
DESERVE ALL OF THIS?

WHY CANT MY LIFE EVER JUST
BE ALRIGHT

THE ANGER NOW HAS PASSED I
GUESS THAT THE PAIN HAS TOO

I FEEL SO EMPTY, LOST, AND
ALONE

MY SOUL WAS GIVEN ALREADY
TO YOU.

# GROWING PAST DEFEATED

SO MANY TIMES THROUGH LIFE I
HAVE HAD MY ASS KNOCKED
DOWN

I WOULD FIEND FOR ANY TYPE OF
CHEMICAL SUBSTANCE

I WOULD DO ANY PILL, DRINK OR
DRUG AROUND

A CONSTANT REPETITION, A
BROKEN RECORD STUCK ON
REPEAT

I WOULD COLLECT MYSELF AND
STAND UP ONCE MORE

ONLY TO ONCFE AGAIN FEELING
DEFEAT

TIMES HAVE CHANGED AND I
HAVE GROWN

I WANT SO MUCH MORE OUT OF
LIFE OTHER THAN ALL IVE EVER
KNOWN.

## TO JUST BE ENOUGH FOR ONE...

SHE WAS BARELY A TEENAGER
WHEN SHE FELT HER FIRST
HEART BREAK

IT WAS THE MOST PAINFUL DUE
TO THE THREE BABIES THAT
LOVE HELPED HER MAKE.

ALL THROUGHOUT HER
TWENTIES

SHE PRETENDED SHE DIDN'T
CARE ABOUT THE PAIN

FLYING THROUGH
RELATIONSHIPS THAT JUST AS
FAST SOON FELL APART

ONLY HEARTACHE WAS THE
GAIN

A WALL WAS BUILT AROUND HER
HEART, TOUGH AND COLD HER
SHELL LOOKED TO THE EYES;

BUT BROKEN AND ACHING AND
LONGING FOR LOVE,

SHE DREAMED OF BEING
ENOUGH FOR JUST ONE GUY.

NOW NEARLY FORTY,
HEARTACHE WAS FAILING AS A
WIFE

A HEARTACHE LIKE NO OTHER

THAT WOULD BE WORTH
STOPPING HER LIFE.

## NERVOUS AND NEW

WHY WOULD HE BE SO
ATTRACTED TO ANYONE WHO
LOOKS LIKE ME?

HE IS HANDSOME, HE IS
HEALTHY, AND HE IS SMART.

A TEXT EVERY SINGLE MORNING
AS HE WAKES UP

ANOTHER AT BEDTIME OR IF WE
ARE EVER APART

WE STARE INTO EACH OTHERS
EYES AS WE PASSIONATELY
MAKE LOVE AGAIN

BOTH HIS AND HER TRACK
RECORD LOOK BAD

IS IT POSSIBLE THAT THIS
TOGETHER THING WILL NOT END

THE BRAND NEW IS STILL THERE

I AM NERVOUSLY TREMBLING
NOT KNOWING WHAT TO DO OR
WHAT TO SAY

AFTER LAST NIGHT'S HEART TO
HEART

I TOLD HIM THAT I LOVE HIM
TODAY.

## STAY

SCARED OF REJECTION

MORE SELF WORTH THAN MANY
READ TO HIM

HOW SHE REALLY FELT

AND THE RESULT WAS THE BEST
OF ANY

AT FIRST HE WIPED THE TEARS
AS THEY FELL DOWN HIS FACE

HE LAY DOWN BESIDE HER ATO
HOLD HER ASKING NOT TO BE
REPLACED.

HE LOVED DIFFERENT THAN HE
HAD BEFORE

ASK ABOUT HER NEEDS THE
NEXT DAY

WITH HONESTY, TRUTH, AND
TRUST,

SHEM MAY HAVE MET THE ONE WHO

COULD ACTUALLY HONESTLY STAY.

## YOUR NAME

NO HAPPINESS

NO LOVE

I AM NOT WORTHY OF JOY

ONLY PAIN

AND I WILL BREAK A LITTLE MORE

EACH TIME THAT I HEAR YOUR NAME.

## COUNTING DAYS

ALTHOUGH TOMORROW WILL
MAKE TEN DAYS SINCE MY
HUSBAND WALKED OFF,

NOT EVEN TO SAY GOODBYE

TODAY HAS MADE NINE DAYS
THAT I HAVE SAT ALL ALONE
AND CRY

TOMORROW WILL BE THE
SECOND TIME THAT HE HAS TO
GO OFF TO JAIL

TODAY, JUST LIKE ANY OTHER,
THE PAIN FROM MISSING HIM
FEELS LIKE HELL

TOMORROW WILL BE THE FIRST
DAY OF THE REST OF MY LIFE

BUT TODAY IS THE LAST DAY
THAT I FEEL AS IF I AM HIS WIFE

I ALREADY FEEL SO LOST AND
LONELY LOCKED AWAY

IN MY ROOM TO HIDE AL THE
PAIN

BUT I HAVE TO GET UP AND
MOVE AROUND ITS ALL PAIN
AND NO GAIN.

## IT MIGHT BE REAL

IT MIGHT BE FUN, OR IT MAY
EVEN BE REAL

WHATEVER IT IS AS LONG AS NO
MORE PAIN IS WHAT I FEEL

TEXTING AND PHOTOS FOR
SEVERAL WEEKS IN

I FEEL COMFORTABLE AS IF YOU
HAVE ALWAYS BEEN A FRIEND

I STOP BY AND BASICALLY SPEND
THE NIGHT

YOU LIGHT A FLAME INSIDE OF
ME

THEN THE FIRST NIGHT, AS QUICK
AS YOU CAME

YOU BLOCKED ME AWAY AND
LEFT ME THIS WAY

ONLY TO SKIP PAST THE
IMPORTANCE THAT TODAY WAS
MY BIRTHDAY

FRIENDS WITH BENEFITS

YET ITS BEEN EVERY DAY SINCE
THEN

I SLIPPED UP AND SAID THAT I
LOVE YOU

YOU SAID ITS OKAY AND
NOTHING ELSE

I WISH THAT I COULD
UNDERSTAND THE THOUGHTS
THAT ARE HELD BY YOU

## MEMORIES LOST

WITH ALL OF THE YEARS THAT
HAVE FLEW ON PAST US BY

SO MANY OF MY MEMORIES HAVE
BECOME LOST ALONG WITH
THEM TOO

BUT ONE THING THAT I CAN
VERY CLEARLY REMEMBER ARE
THE MEMORIES OF A YOUNG
CHILD WITH YOU

LIFE THREW OUT SOME
DISTRACTIONS

OUR CHILDHOODS WERE AT
LILLIE'S AND EVEN MY MAMA'S
TOO

AND THEN WE SOMEHOW
PARTED WAYS UNTIL THE
TRAILER PARK

YOU ALL MOVED IN AND SETUP

MY MIND WAS SOMEWHERE LOST
AND DARK

SHYNESTA WAS CAUGHT IN BED
WITH MY BOYFRIEND

I CRIED SO HARD FOR DAYS

AND MY MAMA ASKED IF I HAD
REMEMBERED CODY

AND I SURE REMEMBERED HIS
TERRIBLE WAYS

ASHLEY AND KACIE FIXED ME UP

A POOR PONYTAIL OFF TO ONE
SIDE

WE WALKED DOWN TO HIS MOM'S
AND I ALMOST WAS SO NERVOUS
THAT I COULD CRY.

HE WAS SO GORGEOUS

WE CHILLED TOGETHER FROM
THAT DAY

THREE CHILDREN LATER ...

I GUESS THAT GOD MADE IT
TURN OUT THAT WAY.

## GOD'S PLAN

IT WASN'T VERY LONG AGO WE
CELEBRATED OUR WEDDING DAY

YOU HAD JUST MADE IT HOME
AFTER EIGHT LONG AND HARD
MONTHS

FOREVER WITH YOU I WANTED
TO STAY

BUT GOD'S PLAN WAS DIFFERENT

YOU RELAPSED WITH A NEEDLE
BACK INTO YOUR ARM

BUT THE SEX SITES YOU
OBSESSED OVER ARE WHAT
DONE ME THE MOST HARM

BILLS ARE ALL PAST DUE AT
THE CUT OFF DATES

AND ME WITHOUT ANY MONEY
COMING IN

I SAT IN MY ROOM FOR ELEVEN
STRAIGHT DAYS CRYING OUT FOR
MY HUSBAND, MY FAMILY, HELL
EVEN JUST A FRIEND

LIFE WAS SMOOTH SAILING

I WAS IN MY COMFORT ZONE

OR MAYBE I WAS NIAVE WITH
ALL OF THE STUFF I HAD NOT
KNOWN

A SLAP TO THE FACE

THE END TO MY LIFE

I VOWED BEFORE GOD FOREVER
FOR BETTER OR WORSE TO BE
HIS WIFE

THE BATTLE IS ONE IM SO
FAMILIAR WITH

THE BLAME MIGHT AS WELL BE
ON ME

I WAS GIVING IT MY ALL, MY
EVERYTHING

AFTER FIVE YEARS WHY
COULDN'T I JUST SEE?

MY WORLD CAME DOWN
CRASHING, THE MONEY HE HAD
ALL BLOWN ON DOPE

THE BILLS THAT HE WAS
SUPPOSED TO HAVE PAID

A JOB, NO MONEY, NO FOOD FOR
THE KIDS WELLL ALSO A NOPE.

WEEK ONE PASSED BY AND I
NEVER LEFT MY ROOM AT ALL

WEEK TWO PASSED AND THE
THOUGHT OF DEATH ENGULFED
ME YET NO WORD FROM HIM
AND STILL NO CALL

NO FAMILY TO VISIT OR TO
CHECK ON ANYTHING

BY THE TIME THAT WEEK THREE
AND FOUR PASSED BY

ID GIVEN AWAY EVERY MEMORY
AND PAWNED THE WEDDING
RING

WEEK FIVE I FOUND A JOB AND A
MAN TO CATCH MY EYE

OH LORD, WHAT IS WRONG WITH
ME

AFTER THIS SHIT I DO NOT NEED
ANOTHER GUY

WEEK SIX I AM RUNNING TO HIM
AND THEN TO A SHITTY JOB TO
SPEND MY TIME

NOW, EIGHT WEEKS, HE IS
REALLY SPECIAL

AND I MIGHT BE MANAGER
AGAIN

AND IM CERTAIN IT IS IN MY
LATE THIRTIES THAT I HAVE HIT
MY PRIME

WORKING ON LEARNING ME
SOMETHING THAT I AM CLUELESS
ON

ILL NEVER RETURN TO BEING
WHO I WAS EVER AGAIN

SHIT CHANGES YOU AND LIFE
GOES ON.

## HEY THERE BRANDON,

HERE WE ARE OUT OF NO
WHERE

YET I FEEL AS IF MY SOUL HAS
KNOWN YOURS FOR YEARS

A CALM TO MY CHAOTIC STORM

A SENSE OF PEACE FROM THE
DEPRESSSION, ANXIETY AND
TEARS

THE MOMENT THAT I LEAVE YOU

MYY HEART HITS MY FEEL AND A
SADNESS I SOON FEEL

TRUST ISSUES AND BAD
RELATIONSHIPS OVERWHELM ME

MY INSECURITIES ARE ALL TOO
REAL

BUT AT THE SAME TIME MY
HEART WANTS TO LET YOU ON IN

I JUST WANTED A CALL OR A
TEXT BACK WHEN I SUGGESTED

THAT WE COULD BE BENEFICIAL
FRIENDS

I CANT JUST BE THAT WITH EACH
NEW TIME I LET YOU INSIDE OF
ME

THE FEELING AND EMOTIONS
GROW STRONGER AND OHHH...

WHAT A FOOL I MIGHT BE

I SLIPPED UP AND SAID THAT I
LOVE YOU

I AM FULLY AWARE THAT IT IS
WAY TOO SOON FOR THAT RIGHT
NOW

BUT MY HEART STILL FEELS IT
LIKE NO OTHER

MY HEART EVER WOULD ALLOW

I KNOW THAT YOU HAVE BEEN
TREATED PRETTY SHITTY

I KNOW THAT WOMEN HAVE
DONE YOU PRETTY BAD

I KNOW, TOO, THAT I HAVE BEEN
LEFT ALONE AND BROKEN
HEARTED

TREATED LIKE OLD GARBAGE
AND TAKEN FOR ALL THAT I
HAD

YOU WONT LET ME IN AND I
QUESTION THE MOTIVES OF YOU

BUT I AM WILLING TO FIVE LOVE
ONE FINAL RUN

THE RESULT IS COMPLETELY UP
TO YOU

IF IT IS BAD ILL BE COMPLETELY
DONE

IM NOT TRYING TO LIVE
TOGETHER AND IM NOT TRYING
TO INTERRUPT YOUR NORMALITY
OR ROUTINE

I JUST WANT TO BE A SMALL
PART OF WHAT YOU CALL YOUR
OWN

I WANT TO HOLD YOUR HAND AS
YOU CONQUER ALL OF YOUR
DREAMS

IF ANYONE ON EARCOULD CHOSE
TO HOLD MY HAND

OVER AND OVER AGAIN IT IS YOU

THAT I WOULD PICK TO BE BY ME

MY SOUL CRAVES YOU EVERY
SECOND THAT YOU ARE NOT
NEAR MY SIDE AND NO CAL OR
CONTACT DRIVES ME SO CRAZY

I SEE YOUR NAME ACROSS MY
PHONE AND I SMILE FROM EAR
TO EAR

THEN I QUESTION THE TRUTH
BEHIND IT ALL

YOU SAY BECAUSE OTHERS LEFT
ME IN FEAR

YOU SAY TO QUIT OVERTHINKING
IT AND LIVE ONE DAY AT A TIME

WELL THAT IS REALLY FUCKING
HARD BECAUSE I AM UNCERTAIN
IF MY HAPPINESS IS ACTUALLY
COMPLETELY MINE

YOU'VE TAKEN ME FROM THE
PAIN THAT I WAS DROWNING IN

YOU'VE BECOME A BEAUTIFUL
DISTRACTION

BUT I CANNOT CALM DOWN AND
STOP WORRYING UNTIL WORDS
BECOME YOUR REACTION

REASSURE ME, BABY, IF YOU
WANT TO GIVE US A REAL TRY
AND SEE WHAT HAPPENS THEN

I NEED TO KNOW WHERE YOUR
MIND AND HEART ARE AT AND
PRAY IT IS MORE THAN A
BENEFICIAL FRIEND.

## HER HEART

HER HEART HAD BEEN BROKEN
B A MAN WHO CAUSED NOTHING
BUT TEARS

HER FRIENDS HAD BECOME FEW
AND FAR BETWEEN

WHILE HES BEEN LOCKED AWAY
NOW SEVEN YEARS

DISTANT AND LONELY

SHE HELD ON TO ANYONE THAT
SHE COULD TOUCH

THE DEPRESSION AND
DARKNESS ENGULFED HER

SHES ALIVE BUT NOT BY MUCH

HE TRIED TO PASS A CAMERA
OFF FOR PORN

AND THEY CHARGED HIM AS IF
HE HAD KILLED

HE WILL MAKE IT THOUGH,

HE IS SO STRONG WILLED

SHE MIGHT HAVE MISSED OUT ON
A CHANCE AT REAL LOVE

BUT THE LONELINESS TOOK
OVER AND SHE HAD TAKEN FAR
TOO ENOUGH.

SHE IS SCARED TO COMMIT FOR
GOD KNOWS HOW MANY MORE
YEARS

EVERY TIME SHE GIVES HER
HEART

THEY ALWAYS LEAVE HER
SHEDDING TEARS.

## TAKE AWAY THE CRAZY

PLEASE BE PATIENT WITH ME AS
I TRY TO LEARN US AS WE GO.

MY MIND KEEPS TELLING ME TO
HAVE DOUBTS AND FEARS

WELL HELL, UNTIL NOW IT IS ALL
THAT IVE EVER SEEMED TO
SHOW.

I GIVE YOU ALL OF ME, 100%
INSIDE AND OUT.

PANICKING WHEN YOUR TEXT
TAKE TOO LONG OR YOU DON'T
SAY I LOVE YOU AND SO I POUT

I WANNA SLAP MYSELF IN THE
FOREHEAD OR TELL MYSELF TO
GET A GRIP

IM SCARED THAT YOU WILL GET
SICK OF ME AND MY TRIPPING
WILL MAKE YOU FLIP

THAT CAUSES THE FEAR AGAIN

REPEAT THE CYCLE, LORD ONLY
KNOWS WHY

PLEASE REMOVE AL OF THIS
CRAZINESS

I FEEL AS IF I COULD CRY.

## NOT BROKEN, NOT SHATTERED

EVERYONE IN THE PAST TURNED
OUT BASICALLY ALL THE SAME

LIES, DRUGS, WHORES, AND
AFFAIRS WITH THE ONLY
DIFFERENCE BEING THEIR
NAMES.

COMING FROM THE SAME CROWD
AND HANGING AROUND WITH
THE VERY SAME CREW

CROSSING EACH OTHERS PATH
MANY TIMES IN OUR PAST,

BUT I HAVE NEVER REALLY
BEFORE MET YOU

I FELL IN LOVE, HEAD OVER
HEELS WITHOUT GIVING IT A
SECOND THOUGHT

I COULD ALMOST SWEAR THAT
YOUD BE THERE IF I HAD
FALLEN,

WELL I THOUGHT

NOW MY HEART IS NUMB, NOT
BROKEN, NOR TORN OR
SHATTERED.

I DON'T HAVE ANY FAITH FOR
ANYTHING ANYMORE BECAUSE I
LOST ALL THAT SEEMED TO
REALLY MATTER.

## WHAT GOES UP MUST COME DOWN

MORE THAN JUST ONCE NOW

YOU'VE SEEN THE VIEW FROM ROCK BOTTOM

YOU'VE ALSO SEEN WHAT IT LOOKS LIKE FROM THE VERY TOP, TOO

GUITARS AND MUSIC, DRUGS, BEER, AND BITCHES WHO WANT A SELFIE

THEY BEG FOR YOUR AUTOGRAPH WHISPERING ABOUT WHAT THINGS TO YOU THEYD DO.

LIKE THE SUN AND GRAVITY

WHAT GOES UP MUST COME DOWN NO MATTER WHAT MY FRIEND

AND IN SILENCE NOW YOU JUST
SIT HERE BESIDE MEASKING
YOURSELF HOW YOU GOT HERE
AGAIN

IT STARTED WITH A BROKEN
HEART

AND LEFT YOU RUNNING
AROUND FEELING NUMB REAL
FASTT

BUT NO SUBSTANCE ON EARTH,
BEER, LIQUOR, PUSSY, OR SPEED
CAN REMOVE THE MEMORIES
THAT REMAIN FROM THE PAST.

IF YOU EVER FIND YOURSELF
CROSSING THAT WICHITA COUNTY
LINE AGAIN IN THE FUTURE
SOME DAY

STOP IN OR CALL ME UP AND I
WILL MAKE THE EFFORT TO
LISTEN TO WHAT YOU SAY

YOU KEEP THE AUTOGRAPHS
AND I LL HOLD ON TO PICTURES
DEAR

DON'T BE AFRAID TO WRITE OR
CALL

BUT MORESO LEARN AGAIN TO
LOVE WITHOUT FEAR.

## TOMORROW

TOMORROW YOU WILL GET IN
YOUR TRUCK

AND I MIGHT NEVER SEE YOU
AGAIN

BUT A SMILE IS ON MY FACE

THINKING OF THE TIME WE
SPENT SO PRICELESS MY FRIEND

NO SILVER OR GOLD, DIAMONDS
OR JEWELS, CARS, CASH OR
CREDIT CARDS

CAN TAKE THE PAIN OUT OF
YOUR HEART AND YOUR
ACTIONS BECAUSE YOU LET THE
PAST TEAR YOU APART.

LET IT GO AND LET GOD DEAL
WITH THEIR SINS

YOU ARE ONLY RESPONSIBLE
FOR YOU

AND REMEMBER YOU ALWAYS
HAVE A FRIEND RIGHT HERE

CODY O'NEIL, I SURE LOVE YOU.

# TIME TO LET GO

NOW WITHIN A FEW SHORT DAYS
AROUND EACH OTHER

THE TIME HAS COME FOR ME TO
LET GO

AS YOUR TRUCK DRIVES AWAY I
QUESTIONIF THE MEMORIES
HAVE FOUND AN END

ID RATHER BE BROKE AND KEEP
TO MYSELF THE MEMORIES THAT
WE HAVE SHARED MY FRIEND

FUCK MONEY GOLD OR SILVER
AND THE CASH OR CARDS THAT
BUY YOU YOUR DREAMS

THE PICTURES ON MY PHONE
AND UNDERSTANDING HOW YOU
HURT

LAUGHIN ALL NIGHT IS MORE
EXTREME

I KNOW THAT I AM NOT ALONE IN
THIS WORLD, THE BLACK SHEEP

IT WASN'T A LOVE TO FILL A VOID

BUT FOREVER A TRUE
FRIENDSHIP I WILL FOREVER
KEEP.

YOU CANNOT RUN FOREVER
FROMM THE PAIN IN YOUR
HEART OR THE THOUGHTS IN
YOUR HEAD YOU CANT GET
DRUNK AND SMOKE MOUNTAINS
OF DOPE

SUN UP TO SUN DOWN AND NOT
FEEL ANYTHING LESS OF BEING
DEAD

IF I HAD MET YOU ANY SOONER
NO COMMON GROUND WE
WOULD SHARE LIKE WE HAVE
DONE LATELY

AND WE ONLY WOULD HAVE A
PASSING GLANCE,

NO FRIENDSHIP AT ALL
BETWEEN YOU AND ME

SO AS YOU CONTINUE TO LEAVE
THIS TOWN RUNNING

TRYING TO OUTRACE THE PAIN
IN YOUR HEART AND IN YOUR
MIND

ILL SIT HERE AND CHERISH THE
MEMORIES THAT ILL BE
FOREVER HOLDING

OR ANOTHER SOUL BADLY
DAMAGED JUST LIKE MYSELF
WILL CONTINUE TO GO ON
LOVING BLIND.

## BILLY

EVERY TIME THAT I CLOSE MY
EYES

MY MIND DRIFTS BACK TO
ANOTHER'S LIES

YOU MAKE ME HAPPIER THAN I
HAVE EVER FET

WHEN YOUR LIPS TOUCH MINE
MY HEART JUST MELTS

WHEN YOU DRIVE AWAY AND I
LAY HERE ALL ALONE

I DWELL ON ALL THE ISSUES
THAT COULD GO WRONG

I CANT SLEEP BABY NOT
WITHOUT YOU HOLDING ME

I CANT SLEEP BABY

I NEED YOU FOR ETERNITY

I DON'T MEAN TO COMPARE YOU
TO THE PUNKS THAT CAME
BEFORE

BUT ITS ALL THAT I HAVE
KNOWN AND NOTHING MORE

I JUST NEED TO TRUST AND WAIT
AND SEE

EVERYTIME THAT I CLOSE MY
EYES,

I CANT SLEEP BABY.

## SHE NASTY SHYNESTA

WELL HELLO MRS. REED

MISS BETTER THAN HER FAMILY
OR HER FRIENDS

YOU ARE CRITICIZING AND
JUDGMENTAL, A HYPOCRIT

AND THE SHIT YOU POSTED ON
FACEBOOK WAS COMPLETE
NONSENSE

I HOPE AND I PRAY THAT
KARMA RAPES YOU IN THE ASS

AND YOU ARE KNOCKED OF
THAT PEDASTOOL YOU ARE ON

AND I PRAY SOMEONE BELITTLES
YOU BY SPREADING LIES AND
RUJMORS TO WHERE YOUR WILL
TO LIVE IS GONE

ILL ASK IF YOU ARE OKAY,

SO COCKY, YOU WILL TRY TO LIE.

NOW YOU KNOW HOW BAD IT
FEELS WHEN ALL YOU WANT
ANYMORE IN LIFE IS TO JUST DIE.

## CHASING MY DREAMS

I THOUGHT THAT WHEN I
MARRIED YOU

IT WOULD BE UNTIL DEATH THAT
WE EVER PART

YOU BROKE OUR VOWS AND
DENIED MY SAY SO ABOUT IT

I SHOULD HAVE KNOWN FROM
THE START

YOU HURT MY FEELINGS AND
HEART MY HEART

YOU CHEATED ON THE PERSON
WHO LOVED YOU MORE THAN
LIFE

BUT WHAT MAKES ABSOLUTELY
NO SENSE TO ME IS IF YOU
PLANNED TO KEEP
DISRESPECTING ME,

WHY DID YOU MAKE ME YOUR WIFE?

I LOST MY PRIDE AND YOU DESTROYED MY SELF ESTEEM

YOU SHATTERED MY HEART NOW SOMEONE ELSE WILL BE BESIDE ME AS I CONTINUE TO CHASE MY DREAMS.

## SMART ASS MOUTH

WELL, I THINK THAT YOU HAVE FINALLY SUCCEEDED AT MAKING ME HATE YOU

FROM BURNING OFF OR TO BRINGING BITCHES AND ACCUSATIONS TOO

I AM NOT SURE WHAT KINDA SCUMBAG BITCHES YOU ROLLED WITH IN THE PAST

BUT TO ACCUSE ME OF FUCKING
YOUR BEST FRIEND, YOU NEED
TO GET OFF OF THE GAS

BUT NOW WHAT THE HELL, WHY
NOT?

IVE ALREADY BEEN ACCUSED OF
SLEEPING WITH HIM TODAY

AND IM DONE FUCKING WITH YOU
AND I WILL NOT BE SEEING YOU
ANYMORE ANYWAY

OH SHIT, HE EVEN CAME BACK
AND SAID THAT HE SHOULD
HAVE STAYED

YOUR SMART ASS MOUTH JUST
HELPED ME GET LAID

## INTIMATE

AS I SLIDE MY HAND DOWN
INSIDE OF MY THIGHS

AND I LET THE VIBRATIONS
OVERWHELM THE LOWER PART
OF ME

I BITE MY LIP AND CLOSE MY
EYES

AND LET YOU JUST TALK

IT WOULD EMBARRASS ME IF
YOU KNEW WHAT I WAS DOING

OR EVEN MORE IF YOU COULD
SEE

I HOLD FIRMLY ON THE GRIP AS I
CARESS SMALL STROKES
AGAINST MY CLIT

GLIDING INSIDE AND OUTSIDE OF
MY BODY

AS A WARM FLUSH THROUGHOUT MY BODY FLOODS OVER ME JUST AS I GET.

WELL YOU ASKED WHY I WAS GIGGLING UT I DON'T HAVE THE NERVE TO COME RIGHT OUT AND SAY

THAT WITHOUT REASONN YOU JUST TURNED ME ON AND ..

WELL...

IM NOT SURE WHAT HAS GOTTEN INTO ME TODAY.

AS I ACCIDENTLY SLIP AND LET OUT THE SLIGHTEST MOAN

I FANTASIZE ABOUT YOU LIKING ME, DIGGING ME, AND COMING HOME.

A RIVER OF HEAT RUNS FROM WITHIN ME AS I LET IT ALL OUT

I CAME TO YOUR VOICE OVER
THE PHONE

BUT KNOW THAT WONT BE THE
CASE WHEN YOU GET OUT

NO ONE EVER HAS MADE ME
FEEL THIS WAY JUST TALKING ON
A PHONE.

I CAN IMAGINE MYSELF PRESSED
AGAINST YOUR SKIN

ONE BODY BECOMES FROM US
TWO.

GOOD LORD LET HIM GET OUT
AND COME HOME

LET HIM AND I SHARE A LOVE
THAT IS TRUE.

## MY OLDEST SON

I KNOW THAT I HAVENT BEEN
THE WORLDS GREATEST
MOTHER

BUT I TRY AT LEAST TO BE A
GOOD FRIEND

I LISTEN AND LOVE LIKE NO
OTHER

ILL STAND BESIDE YOU UNTIL
THE END

I WATCH YOU PUT EVERY OUNCE
OF YOUR SOUL INTO WHAT YOU
LOVE

AND I NOTICE AS YOU ARE
SHORT CHANGED ALL THAT YOU
ARE TRULY WORTH

ALTHOUGH YOU CANNOT
RECOGNIZE IT YOURSELF

I KNEW YOU WERE SPECIAL
SINCE THE DAY THAT I GAVE
BIRTH

IT BREAKS MY HEART THAT MY
GRANDDAUGHTER DOES NOT
KNOW WHO I AM

BUT IT IS NO ONE'S FAULT OTHER
THAN MY OWN

I LET MY PITY PARTY SEPARATE
ME FROM MY FAM.

I WILL GET BACK LIKE I NEED TO

THIS WORLD DOESN'T CARE AND
IT'S A FACT

I NEED THE ATTENTION
DEVOTED TO YALL AGAIN

BECAUSE THAT'S THE ONLY
PLACE WHERE MY HAPPINESS IS
AT

## HAYDEN

I REMEMBER THE DAY THAT I
BROUGHT YOU HOME

YOUR BROTHER SAID TO THROW
YOU INTO THE TRASH AND HE
CRIED

NOW I TEAR UP WATCHING YOU
TWO GROW SO CLOSE

I LOVE THAT IN EACH OTHER
THE TWO OF YOU CONFIDE

I REMEMBER AT JUST A COUPLE
OF WEEKS OLD

YOU CAME DOWN WITH RSV

I COULDN'T BARE THE THOUGHT
OF LOSING YOU

I SAT AT THE HOSPITAL AND I
CRIED

DESPERATELY YOU GREW
STRONGER AND YOU TOUGHT ME
TO FIGHT JUST LIKE YOU DID

AND THE STRENGTH THAT YOU
HAVE GIVEN ME

IS ALL BECAUSE THE STRENGTH I
LEARNED FROM YOU, MY KID.

NOW THAT I LAY HERE ALL
ALONE

A MILLION THOUGHTS THAT
CLOUD MY MIND YOU SEE

I GAVE EVERYTHING THAT I HAD
SO THOUGHT TO A MAN

WHEN THEY ALL JUST LEAVE
EVENTUALLY

BUT THAT IS JUST WRONG I HAVE
SO MUCH MORE

LOVE AND DEVOTION IN ME FOR
THE THREE OF YOU

I GAVE BIRTH TO LEAVEN BUT
HAYDEN MEANS THE WORLD
TOO

NO MATTER HOW THIS WORLD
ACTS AS YOU BECOME WHO YOU
WANT TO BE

BE YOU, GIVE IT YOUR ALL,
EVERYTHING THAT YOU GOT

BECAUSE YOU WILL ALWAYS BE
PERFECT TO ME.


## DUSTIN

IM NOT SURE WHAT YOU MIGHT
BE THINKING

BECAUSE YOU WONT EVER TALK
ABOUT THINGS WITH ME

BUT I UNDERSTAND MORE THAN
YOU GIVE ME CREDIT FOR

YOU ARE MY MINI ME YOU SEE

YOU BOTTLE UP YOUR WORRIES,
YOUR CARES, AND CONCERNS

UNTIL IT OVERWHELMS YOUR
MIND

ITS NOT HEALTH AT ALL SO LET
IT ALL OUT

IM HERER TO LISTEN, THE BEST
LISTENER THAT YOU WILL EVER
FIND

IM SORRY FOR WHO IVE BECOME
LATELY

IVE SHUT DOWN WITH LIFE WITH
WHAT CODY DID

I RAN AND I LASHED OUT
HURTING MYSELF AND ALL
THREE OF YOU KIDS

YOU NEED ME JUST OR EVER
MORE THAN WHAT I NEED OF
YOU

JUST DON'T EVER GIVE UP NO
MATTER WHAT YOU CHOSE TO
DO

MY MIDDLE CHILD, MY MINI ME,
THE BOY WITH SUCH A SIMILAR
SOUL

I WILL TRY HARDER TO BECOME
BETTER

AND I LOVE YOU FOREVER,
DON'T YOU KNOW?

### ROBBIN'

BEFORE I ACTUALLY GOT TO
KNOW YOU

YOU RAN A PRETTY GOOD GAME

BUT I OBSERVE WHAT IS GOING
ON AROUND ME

AND YOUR MOTIVE IS BASICALLY
THE SAME

YOUR HUSTLE IS TO BOUNCE
BACK AND FORTH BETWEEN
FEMALES

USING THEM FOR DOPE AND
MONEY

YOU USE THEM UNTIL THERE IS
NOTHING LEFT FOR YOU TO TAKE

AND THEN ITS ON TO THE NEXT
ONE THINKING IT IS FUNNY

THE NERVE TO ASK IF ID GET
YOU AND YOUR WHORE HIGH
FOR THE DAY

YOU, ALONE, WAS ONE THING,

BUT A BITCH TOO...

DON'T PLAY

I FELL AT FIRST FOR YOUR
CHARM

AND THERE WAS NOT A
SHORTAGE OF MEAT IN THE
ROOM,

KNOW WHAT I MEAN?

BUT THAT HYPNOSIS WAS FADED
OFF ALREADY AND SOME LITTLE
POCKED ROBBING PRICE NO
LONGER FAZES THIS QUEEN

SO HAVE YOUR WAY WITH THE
NIAVE HOES

AND KEEP THINKING WHAT YOU
ARE DOING IS COOL

BUT WHEN IT IS ALL SAID AND
DONE AND THEY CATCH ON

YOU WILL BE THE ONE LEFT
ACTING LIKE A FOOL.

## OTHER SIDE OF THE TRACKS

SHE AINT NEVER CAME FROM
MONEY

SHE IS FROM THE OTHER SIDE OF
THE TRACKS

YOU CAN KEEP YOUR WORLDLY
POSSESSIONS

BECAUSE YOU CANT TAKE THEM
WHEN YOU GO, THAT A FACT

WHAT HAPPENED TO BEING
HUMBLE

OR LOVE YOUR NEIGHBOR AND
TO THY SELF BE TRUE

YOURE FOCUSED ON "HE HAS
MORE THAN ME"

YOU WANT WHAT YOU WANT
WHEN YOU WANT IT TO DO

WHEN IT IS ALL SAID AND DONE
AND SHE WILL BE LEFT WITH
ENVY AND GREED, NO MORE

AND SHE WLL HAVE A JEWEL IN
HER CROWN

SHE WILL ENTER HEAVEN FULL
OF LOVE

AND YOU....WELL ITS HOT FOR
WHAT YOU WILL HAVE COMING IN
STORE

## <u>PB&J</u>

MY HEART WAS SHATTERED BY
SOMEONE CAUSING SO MANY
TEARS

YOU HAE LOST A FEW FRIENDS
WHILE LOCKED AWAY

THESE YEARS

THEY SAY I AM DISTANT
DEPRESSED AND SUCH

I ADMIT WHEN THEY SAY THAT
THE LAST FEW MONTHS HAVE
BEEN TOO MUCH

OUR FRIEND SAYS THAT NOW
YOU SEEM EXCITED AND WELL

AND YOU JOIN HIM EACH TIME
HE GOES TO CHECK EMAIL

THE DARKNESS AND
DEPRESSION HAVE UP AND
CLEARED AWAY

THE ONLY TIME THAT I FEEL SAD
WAS WHEN I DIDN'T TALK TO YOU
THAT DAY

I LOVE THE SOUND OF YOUR
CHUCKLE

IVE LAUGHED AND SMILED
AGAIN TOO

HURRY UP AND SEND THE
PAPER FOR ME TO SIGN

SO I CAN RUN MY ASS TO SEE
YOU

I DON'T BELIEVE EITHER OF US
KNOW WHAT WE HAVE STARTED

WE DAMN SURE DON'T KNOW
WHERE IT MIGHT END

BUT AS FOR NOW I KNOW THAT I
NEED YOU

NEITHER OF US HAVE TO
PRETEND

WE CAN LEAVE BEHIND THE
CHAOS

AND PLAN AHEAD IT SEEMS

ONLY A VOICE AND SOME WORDS
AND A PHOTO

YET I FIND YOU IN MY DREAMS

## THIS SHIT HERE

SOMETIMES I GET A LITTLE
OVERWHELMED WITH MY
SITUATION PHYSICALLY

AND I FRANTICALLY AM LOSING
MY MIND AND TRYING TO EASE
THE PAIN

HOW DID I END UP LIKE THIS
AND NOT ABLE TO STOP IT?

WHY DIDN'T THAT LITTLE LIGHT
COME ON IN MY BRAIN

WERE THERE ANY GOOD
DECISIONS MADE OUT OF THE
LAST FIVE OR SIX YEARS

OBVIOUSLY NOT, BECAUSE EVERY
MEMORY I RECALL

ONLY BRINGS ME TO TEARS

GOD, JUST HELP PULL ME
THROUGH THIS UNTIL I CAN
OVERCOME WHAT IT IS THAT IF
FEEL

I WANT TO LIVE MY LIFE AGAIN

AND FORGET THIS SHITTY
ORDEAL.

THIS PAIN THAT I AM ENDURING
IS NEVERENDING

NO IMPROVEMENT AHEAD IN
SIGHT

ITS CONSTANT AND
UNBEARABLE

IM STARTING TO GIVE UP ON THIS
FIGHT

AND I CANNOT STAND UP
STRAIGHT

MUSCLE CRAMPS KEEP MY
THIGHS ACHING ALL THE WAY
AROUND

SO THERE IS NOT EVER ANY
COMFORT SITTING DOWN OR
STANDING

AND DAMN SURE NOT LAYING

IT IS REALLY PULLING ME DOWN.

## FULL OF FALSE HOPE

HERE LATELY I HAVE BEEN IN
AN ONCOMING DEPRESSION

FULL OF CONFUSION, THIS CHAOS
LEAVES ME ANGRY INSIDE

MY MOODS ARE BASED UPON MY
EMOTIONS

HOT AND COLD, DAY AND NIGHT

I TRY TO CONVINCE MYSELF THAT
ALL OF THE ANGER AND RAGE

ARE JUST A RESULT FROM ALL
OF THE STRESS THAT I HAVE
AND IT IS DUE TO ALL THE PAIN.

BUT THAT IS NOT THE ONLY
REASON THAT I FEEL THIS WAY

I AM ALSO OVERWHELMED WITH
IT ALL COMPLETELY AND IT IS
DRIVING ME INSANE.

RIGHT NOW WE HAVE NOT A
SINGLE BITE IN THE HOUSE TO
EAT

THE BANK IS WAY PAST
INSUFFICIENT FUNDS AND HAS
STAYED THAT WAY

I WORRY IF THE BILLS HAVE ALL
GOTTEN PAID ON TIME

AND WHAT WILL I FEED THE KIDS
FOR DINNER ANOTHER DAY

YOU JUST TELL ME NOT TO
WORRY ABOUT IT BECAUSE IT
WILL ALL SOMEHOW BE OKAY

BUT OVER AND OVER THE SAME
WORRIES ARE WHAT I STRESS ON
AND YOU ACT LIKE IT IS JUST
ANOTHER DAY

IT IS ALWAYS THAT SOMEONE
OWES YOU MONEY AND THEY
WILL NOT SEEM TO PAY YOU OR
WHAT WE HAVE DOESN'T
STRETCH AS FAR AS WE MIGHT
NEED

AND I AM SO FUCKING TIRED OF
CONSTANT STRESS AND
STRUGGLE OVER THE SAME SHIT
AND ITS MAKING ME LOSE MY
MIND AND MY HEART BLEED

HERE LATELY I HAVE BEEN
WITHDRAWN FROM YOU AND

FULL OF ANGER AND
DISAPPOINTMENT TOWARDS YOU
TOO

NO MATTER THE
CIRCUMSTANCES OR WHAT THE
TOPIC MIGHT BE

I FEEL THAT THE ONLY THING
YOU WORRY OR STRESS OVER
AND YOUR ONLY CONCERN IS
YOU.

I TELL MYSELF THAT IF YOU LOVE
ME WITH HALF OF WHAT YOU SAY
THAT YOU DO

YOU WOLD CARE ABOUT MY
WORRIES, MY STRESS, AND MY
PAIN.

THEN I GET UPSET WITH MYSELF
BECAUSE I SEE IM JUST
SEARCHING FOR SOMEONE WITH
A REASON TO BLAME

I HAD IT IN MY HEAD THAT
WHEN MY LIFE WAS SOMEWHAT
ON TRACK THAT ALL OF MY
WORRIES AND TROUBLES WOULD
MAGICALLY DISAPPEAR.

NOW THAT I SEE I FILLED MYSELF
UP WITH A FALSE HOPE

THESE ISSUES, NOW SOBER, HAVE
JUST BECOME TO ME MORE
CLEAR

AND I KNOW HELL OR HIGH
WATER WE WILL GET BY AND WE
WILL MANAGE TO MAKE IT
AGAIN COME NEXT WEEK, WE
ALWAYS DO

I JUST DON'T WANT TO BE THE
FAILURE THAT I ONCE BEFORE
WAS

IN MY KIDS EYES

SO I OBSESS ON IT LIKE ITS
SOMETHING NEW

I JUST KNOW SOMETHING HAS TO
GIVE BECAUSE I AM MAKING
MYSELF MISERABLE AND
DEPRESSED REALLY BAD

JUST A LITTLE RELIEF IS ALL I
AM LONGING FOR

A LITTLE COMFORT FROM IT WILL
KEEP ME FROM GETTING MAD.


## DIFFERENT

IT COULD HAVE BEEN DIFFERENT

IT DIDN'T HAVE TO END THIS
WAY

YEAH, IT COULD HAVE ALL BEEN
SO DIFFERENT

I GUESS THIS IS THE PRIIE I HAVE
TO PAY

I COULD HAVE LIVED A LITTLE
DIFFERENT

BUT THEN AGAIN, THAT LIFE
MADE ME BECOME STRONG

MY CHOICES SHOULD HAVE BEEN
COMPLETELY DIFFERENT

NOW I LIVE LIFE TO MAKE RIGHT
SO MANY WRONGS

WHAT IF LIFE HAD TURNED OUT
SO MUCH DIFFERENT

WHOULD I STILL HAVE LIVED
THROUGH SO MUCH PAIN

MAYBE MY PRIORITIES WERE ON
SOMETHING DIFFERENT

MY LIFE WOULDN'T HAVE BEEN
SO INSANE

IN THE BEGINNING, A LOW SELF
ESTEEM MADE ME DIFFERENT

I WAS RIDICULED BECAUSE OF
MY WEIGHT

IF I HAD HANDLED IT ANY
DIFFERENT

MAYBE I WOULD HAVE LOVE FOR
MYSELF INSTEAD OF HATE

THE REASON MY LIFE IS
DIFFERENT

ALL BASES BACK ON THE
DECISIONS WHEN I WAS YOUNG
AND CAREFREE

IF I HAD ONLY CARED A LITTLE
DIFFERENT

WELL...

I GUESS I WOULDN'T HAVE
BECOME MY OWN DESTINY.

## STRESSIN

IF YOU DON'T MIND

ID LIKE TO BORROW YOUR EAR

THERES SOME THINGS WEIGHING
UPON MY MIND AND HEART

AND YOU ACT AS IF YOU DON'T
NOTICE MY DEPRESSION

OR THAT I SLEEP ALL DAY AND
YOUR NEGLIGENCE BREAKS ME
APART

I STRESS EVERY DAY ON MONEY
AND FOOD

THE BILLS AND WHAT IS IN THE
BANK AGAIN

YOU JUST SAY THAT IT WILL BE
OKAY AND TOMORROW WILL BE
JUST LIKE TODAY ...IT NEVER
ENDS

IM LOSING MY MIND THRYING TO
MAKE IT EACH DAY

YOU JUST LET ME AS IF YOU DO
NOT REALLY CARE

I WISH THAT YOUD SEE THAT ITS
KILLING ME

AND MY STRESS JUST DOESN'T
SEEM TO BE A BOTHER TO
SHARE


## WHAT MADE YOU HATE ME?

I KEEP ASKING MYSELF I NEED
TO KNOW

WHAT ID DID THAT WAS SO BAD
FOR YOU TO HATE ME SO

WAS IT SOMETHING I DID OR WAS
IT SOMETHING I COULDVE SAID

TOO MAKE YOUR LOVE FOR EME
TURN INTO HATRED INSTEAD

DID YOUR FEELINGS CHANGE
OVERNIGHT OR DID YOU JUST
ONE DAY DECIDE YOU LOVED ME
NO MORE

WAS IT ME OR WAS IT BECAUSE
OF SOMETHING YOU MIGHT HAVE
DONE

AND YOU COULDN'T TAKE IT
BACK ONCE YOU HAD?

WAS MY LOVE AND LOYALTY TOO
OVERWHELMING FOR YOU

COULD MY HEART AND SOULD
REALLY BE THAT BAD

IS THERE A CHANCE THAT THIS
HATRED MIGHT FADE AWAY?

DO YOU THINK THAT YOU COULD
EVER AGAIN LOVE ME AND YOU

CHANGE YOUR MIND AGAIN I
PRAY

I WILL ALWAYS LOVE YOU AND IM
SORRY IF I DESTROYED ANY
COMMITMENT THAT YOU ONCE
GAVE

I DON'T THINK THAT I COULD
EVER HATE YOU

WHETHER OUR LOVE CAN OR
CANNOT HAVE A CHANCE TO BE
SAVED

SO JUST KNOW YOU ARE MY
EVERYTHING

YOU WERE MY EVERYTHING
THAT HELD ME IN ONE PIECE

BUT TO KEEP MY SANITY

I HAVE TO LET YOU GO.

CAUSING NOTHING OTHER THAN
A BITTERSWEET RELEASE

SO TOMORROW, NEXT WEEK, OR
EVEN IN TEN YEARS

FROM NOW JUST THE SAME TO
ME EITHER WAY

MY LOVE FOR YOU IS STRONG
AND ILL FOREVER HOLD ON

HOPING ONE DAY AGAIN YOU
MIGHT REMEMBER AND YOUR
HEART WILL BE MINE AGAIN TO
STAY

## ANGRY

IM TRYING TO DECIDE WHAT IT IS
WITH ME THAT MAKES ME HOT
AND COLD

WHAT FLIPS THE SWITCH INSIDE
OF MY MIND AND I FILL WITH
ANGER BY THE TRUCKLOAD

EVERY MOVE, EVERY SOUND,
ALL THAT YOU MIGHT SAY

GETS ON MY NERVES AND I GET
ANGRY INSIDE AND IM NOT SURE
WHAT MAKES ME THIS WAY

I GO TO SLEEP AND WHEN I
AWAKE

IM CALM AND LOVE YOU SO
MUCH ONCE AGAIN

IT PUZZLES ME WHAT WEIGHS
ON MY MIND SO HEAVY THAT
THIS WILL NOT END?

## IN A HURRY TO MAKE IT END

ILL BE THE FIRST ONE  TO ADMIT
THAT IVE SEEN DAYS ON ROCK
BOTTOM

DARK, COLD, AND EMPTY AFTER
IT HAD DRAINED THE LIFE OUT
OF ME

WHEN I HEAR THE SONG
AMAZING GRACE I START TO
WEEP JUST KNOWING I WAS LOST
BUT NOW AM FOUND YOU SEE...

I AM ENTIRELY CERTAIN THAT IM
HERE TODAY ENTIRELY BECAUSE
OF GOD'S GRACE

IF I FEEL ANYMORE ALONE I
KNOW WITHOUT DOUBT

THAT ID LOSE MY LIFE IN THE
RAT RACE

THAT LAST AND FINAL WEEK I
KNEW THAT I WAS DONE WITH IT
ALL IT JUST TOOK ME TWENTY
YEARS BEFORE ALL MY FIGHT
WAS GONE

ALONG WITH ELEVEN GRAND,
THE LOVE FOR A MAN, AND A
BROKEN BACK LEFT LAYING ON
THE LAWN

A THOUSAND TIMES IVE BEEN
TOLD THAT WHAT DOESN'T KILL
YOU MAKES YOU STRONGER

WELLL I WENT FROM STRONGER
INTO A JUNKIE BROKEN DOWN
AND WEAK

WHAT REMAINED WAS A
BROKEN HEART AND A BROKEN
BACK AND A BEATEN SOUL
SCREAMING NO MORE WILL I BE
DEFEAT

I AM SEARCHING FOR A REASON
THAT IM STILL HERE ON EARTH

BECAUSE THERE HAS TO BE A
REASON GOD LET ME LIVE

I HELD MYSELF CAPTIVE INSIDE
OF MY OWN HOME CRYING IN A
RECLINER GIVING UP ON ALL
THAT WAS POSITIVE

IVE BEGGED THE LORD TO TAKE
AWAY THIS PAIN THAT I COULD
NOT CONTROL IT

NO RELIEF UNTIL IM
OVERWHELMED WITH FEAR.

THE PAIN IS IMPOSSIBLE TO
ADJUST TO

TWO MONTHS AGO I HAD BEEN
HURTING NOW A SOLID YEAR

BUT REGARDLESS IT COULD
HAVE BEEN SO MUCH WORSE

THIS IS THE LAST MONTH OF
HELL NONETHELESS

BUT I LOOK UP AT THE SKY AND
LET OUT A PAINFUL SIGH

AND THANK GOD FOR ALL THOSE
THINGS IN WHICH IM BLESSED

IVE WASTED SO MUCH OF MY LIFE
ABUSED BY PUNKS, OR BY A
NEEDLE PIERCING MY SKIN

AMIDST THE CHANGE I LONG TO
SMILE TO FEEL THE NEGATIVE
COME TO AN END

MY LIFE FEELS LIKE IM LIVING
OUT A DRAMATIC HEART
WRENCHING NOVEL

PAGE AFTER PAGE FULL OF
MISTAKE AFTER MISTAKE AGAIIN

I DON'T WAN TO QUESTION
MYSELF IF IM HAPPY

I WANT THOSE DAYS TO DIE SO I
CAN LIVE AND LET LIFE BEGIN

I MIGHT APPEAR OR COME
ACROSS AS SELFISH

BEING ALONE CRYING IN PAIN

I TRULY KNOW THAT THERE ARE
SO MANY PEOPLE WHO CARE

BUT THEN AGAIN IVE SPENT SIX
EXCRUCIATING WEEKS FROM HOT
BATHS TO SLEEPING IN A CHAIR

PEOPLE ARE PROBABLY FED UP
HEARING MY BULLSHIT AMONGST
THEIR OWN

I AM TRULY SICK OF HEARING
MYSELF YOU SEE

I DOONT WANT TO BE ANYTHING
LIKE PERFECTION

I JUST WANT TO MEAN IT WHEN I
SAY IM OK AND NOT IN PAIN
CONSTANTLY.

NOW DAMN IT, I GUESS ILL EAT
THE WORDS THAT I JUST SAID

I GUESS MY STRENGTH COMES
FROM THE MENTAL AND
EMOTIONAL FATIGUE THAT IVE
LATELY FELT

I KNOW LIFE ISNT EVER PERFECT
I JUST DON'T WANT THE PAIN
THAT IVE BEEN DEALT

I WANT TO TAKE MY KIDS FOR A
WALK IN THE ARK AND PUT
ONMY OWN UNDERWEAR
WITHOUT HELP EVERY DAY

HEAVEN IS PLAYING MAMA TO
ME WHICH ISNT FAIR AT ALL

AT ELEVEN YEARS OLD, SHE
SHOULD RUN AROUND AND PLAY

IM JUST RIDING THIS OUT NOT
ADDING FUEL TO THE FIRE

WHEN I GET BETTER, ILL FEEL
MORE WORTHY AND FEEL
WANTED AGAIN

SOMEONE HIS HEART STILL
DESIRES

IM NOT SURE BUT THE WAY THAT
WE ARGUE AND FIGHT

I THINK THAT ITS JUST THE
WORD LOVE THAT REMAINS
TRUE

I BITCH AND I BEG TO BE HELD
UNTIL I AM BLUE IN THE FACE

BUT DAY AFTER DAY THERE'S NO
CHANGE

I FEEL FAT, UGLY AND CRIPPLED
TOO

HE REASSURES ME WITH
WHATEVER, I DO LOVE YOU

THEN HE ROLLS OVER AND
QUICKLY FALLS ASLEEP

ILL LAY FOR HOURS AND TOSS
AND TURN

I WALK AROUND BECAUSE MY
LEGS BURN

A CONVIENIENT WAY TO HIDE
THE TEARS THAT I WEEP

ID RATHER BE ALONE THAN TO
FEEL THIS LONELY

BUT HE CANNOT FIX WHAT I FEEL
DEEP DOWN INSIDE

LAST ATTEMPT AT SEX REALLY
HURT ME, NO PRETEND

BUT JUST HIS SKIN NEXT TO MINE
IS COMFORT LAYING SIDE BY SIDE

ON TOP OF EVERYTHING ELSE IM
LOSING MY BEST FRIEND

WHAT IS NEXT AFTER THESE
TRIBULATIONS AND TESTS THAT
GOD HAS IN FRONT OF ME

WILL THE PAIN AND HEART
ACHE BE ONE AND HAPPINESS I
FEEL AT LAST OR IS THAT JUST A
FANTASY

IM TIRED OF BEING BROKEN AND
SICK OF FEELING PAIN

I WANT TO BE CONTENT, JUST
SATISFIED

IM TIRED OF CONSTANTLY GOING
INSANE.

## THIS PAIN I FEEL

TONIGHT I SIT HERE, ALONE AND
LOST IN MY OWN CHAOTIC
THOUGHTS

IVE CAME TO ADMIT THAT IM
CONFUSED IN MORE WAYS THAN
JUST ONE

I AM A WALKING
CONTRADICTION AND IM SCARED
THERES NO FORGIVENESS FOR
THE THINGS THAT IVE DONE

IM ONE HUNDRED PERCENT
SURE OF ONE THINGG AND
THAT'S IM NOT REAL CERTAIN
ON WHAT TO DO AT ALL

ITS ALMOST BECOME A
PARANOIA BY NOW

AFTER SO MANY TIMES THAT
OTHERS LET ME FALL

LATELY IVE ASKED MYSELF AT
LEAST A HUNDRED TIMES

WHATS THE REASON OR LESSON
GOD HAS BEHIND ALL OF THIS
PAIN?

BECAUSE ITS NEARLY
UNBEARABLE AND TOO
EXTREME NOT TO HAVE A
PURPOSE

I JUST DON'T SEE ANYTHING LEFT
TO GAIN

IT TEARS ME AWAY FROM LIFE
AND IT MAKES ME LAY DOWN IN
TEARS

NO ONE TRULY UNDERSTANDS
HOW BAD THE PAIN IS THAT I
FEEL AND TO FOREVER BE LIKE
THIS I DO FEAR

EVERY POSSIBLE OBSTACLE HAS
BEEN IN THE WAY OF ME
GETTTING BETTER  OR HAVING
SURGERY

EVERY RESPONSE THAT I GET
DENIED AND MY DEPRESSION
GETS THE BEST OF ME

IM MAKING MY FAMILY
MISERABLE

WITH ALL OF MY BITCHING AND
COMPLAINING AND PLUS THE
PAIN

PLEASE LORD EASE MY MIND
AND FIX MY BACK CALM MY
MIND BEFORE I GO INSANE

## LORD

LORD, I KNOW THAT YOU ARE
WITH ME

PLEASE HELP TAKE THIS PAIN
FROM ME

IM LOSING THOUGHT OF ALL
THAT I AM BLESSED FOR

AND LIFES COMPLETELY MISERY

I DON'T KNOW WHAT TRIAL OR
TRIBULATION WOULD CAUSE
YOUR CHILD SO MUCH ANGUISH
AND PAIN

BUT AT LEAST TELL ME THAT I
PASSED IT WITH FLYING COLORS

SUCH A PRICE FOR WHAT TO
GAIN??

I MORE SO HERE LATELY JUST
WANT TO GIVE UP ALL THE WAY

IM SO TIRED OF FEELING THIS
BURNING AND CRAMPING THAT
COMES AND CONSTANTLY STAYS

## GIVEN UP IT SEEMS

HELLO.. DO YOU HEAR ME

CAN YOU SEE ME OVER HERE

YOU GO INTO A COMPLETELY
DIFFERENT ROOM

OR LAY ON THE EDGE OF THE
BED IN FEAR

HEAVEN FORBID THAT I MIGHT
TOUCH YOU

OR HELL, EVEN WANT YOU TO
TOUCH ME

IT BREAKS MY HEART FEELING
THIS ALONE WORSE THAN THE
PAIN IN MY LEGS AND BACK
CONSTANTLY

WHY ARE YOU HERE IF YOU
DON'T LOVE ME

AND IF YOU LOVE ME I DON'T SEE
ANY SIGN TO PROVE ITS TRUE

ITS OVERWHELMING THE
LONELINESS PAIN PHYSICALLY
AND EMOTIONALLY TOO

NOT WORTH A KISS OR A
CUDDLE AT NIGHT

DISTANT THROUGHOUT THE DAY

I DON'T THINK THAT I HAVE HAD
A REASON WORTH LIVING
ANYMORE IT HURTS ANYTHING
THAT I DO OR DO NOT SAY.

## <u>WORTH THE FIGHT</u>

EXCUSE ME MR. GLASSCOCK

FOR THE ANGER AND HATRED IT
SEEMS IVE BEEN GIVING YOU

I TRULY DON'T MEAN TO BE LIKE
THAT BUT THE PAIN IS MAKING
ME HATE EVERYTHING IN LIFE
WITH ALL I DO

I PROMISE I TRULY LOVE YOU
AND I DON'T WANT TO THROW US
AWAY

AFTER ALL THAT WE HAVE BEEN
THROUGH YOU SEE

I GET SCARED THAT WE WILL
NOT MAKE IT OUT AND STILL BE
TOGETHER

I DON'T WANT TO LIVE IF YOU
ARE NOT LIVING LIFE WITH ME

SO AS YOU GRIT YOUR TEETH
AND CLINCH YOUR FIST

ILL TRY MY DAMNEST TO WATCH
MY WORDS AND ATTITUDE THAT
I GIVE YOUR WAY

IT IS WAS EASY IT WOULD NOT BE
WORTH IT, RIGHT?

I'D FIGHT SATAN HIMSELF TO
MAKE YOU STAY

## PLEASE BE PATIENT

I JUST WANT TO TAKE A
MOMENT TO TELL YOU THAT I
AM TRULY SORRY FOR THE HELL
I PUT YOU THRU

YOU GO TO WORK AND TRY YOUR
BEST HERE AT HOME

BUT I FAIL TO APPRECIATE THE
THINGS YOU DO

ALL IT EVER IS FROM ME IS PAIN
FROM THAT BITCHING AND EVEN
TEARS

BUT IM FORGETTINNG THAT IT
COULD ALWAYS BE WORSEAND
THAT IM GRATEFUL THAT AT
LEAST IM STILL HERE

I GET DISGUSTED WITH MYSELF
AND IN RETURN I GET THAT WAY
WITH YOU

WITHOUT EVEN A REASON TO BE
THAT WAY

YOU RIDE IT OUT UNTIL IM
THROUGH

I AM TRULY GRATEFUL FOR YOU
IN MY LIFEAND IN MY DREAMS
THE SAME

NO ONE ELSE COULD EVER
HANDLE ME EXCEPT FOR YOU SO
IT SEEMS

IF YOU CAN BARE WITH ME ILL
GET BETTER SOON I PRAY

AND THEM WE CAN SHARE
SMILES AND LAUGHTER FOR THE
REST OF OUR DAYS.

# ANGRY AT THE WORLD, NOT AT YOU

THANK YOU, MR. GLASSCOCK,

FOR SOMEHOW FINDING A WAY
TO LOVE CRAZY ASS ME

YOU MEAN THE WORLD TO ME
THOUGH I DO NOT SHOW IT

LIFE WITHOUT YOU WOULD BE
PURE MISERY

I BEG FOR YOU TO HOLD ME AND
GET ANGRY IF YOU DON'T TRY

A MILLION MILES AWAY WITHOUT
A KISS OR A TOUCH OR A
WHISPER

I ROLL OVER TO GO TO SLEEP
AND CRY

I WISH YOU WERE STILL IN LOVE
WITH ME

I WISH YOU NEEDED ME LIKE
ONCE YOU SEEMED LIKE YOU
TRULY DID BEFORE

I MISS YOUR ARMS AND LIPS
AGAINST ME

AND NOW YOU DO NOT LOVE ME
ANYMORE

I KNOW IM FAT AND CANNOT
MOVE VERY WELL

AND IT MUST BE BORING NOW TO
YOU

IT HURST TO THINK YOU ARE
DISGUSTED AT ME

AND I DO NOT KNOW WHAT I CAN
POSSIBLY DO..

## CODY AND DESTINY GLASSCOCK

CRAZY WE MUST BE TO EVEN
TRY

ONLY BAD CAN BECOME OF THIS
IT SEEMS

DETERMINED TO MAKE US LAST
FOREVER

YOU ARE THE ONLY MAN I WANT
IN MY DREAMS

ANGRY THAT WE HAVE BEEN
DOWN AND

NEARLY DRUG THROUGH HELL
AND BACK

DON'T IT FEEL THAT WAY AT
LEAST


DEPRESSING AND SAD I FEEL
FROM

EVERY PART INSIDE, BROKEN
AND

SORE NOT AN OUNCE OF PEACE

TELL ME HOW TERRIBLE LIFE

IS NOW FOR YOU

NOW YOU WOULD LOVE TO SAY

YOUR GOODBYES


GUESS YOU CANT WIN FROM
LOSING

LUCK NO WHERE YOUR WAY

ANY LONGER

SO WHICH IS WORSE ALONE OR

SO MANY TEARS THAT MY EYES
CRY

COULDN'T YOU JUST LOVE ME

OR COULD YOU JUST PRETEND

CANT WE ACT LIKE YOU LOVE ME
AND

KEEP US FROM COMING TO AN
END?

# AT HER BITTER END

SHE NEVER REALLY FIT IN WITH
THE CROWD

NO MATTER HOW HARD THAT
SHE TRIED

SHE EITHER TALKED TO FAST OR
LOUD IT SEEMED TO ME

OR THERE WAS JUST PLAIN OLD
DRAMA FROM SOME SNOTTY KID

WHO LOVED TO START SHIT
INSTEAD OF JUST LET HER BE

THEY'D SMILE TO HER FACE AND
SMIRK BEHIND HER BACK SO
MEAN FOR THEM TO BE

NOTHING SHE SAID OR DONE
WOULD HELP HER FIT IN

SHE FINALLY GOT TIRED OF
BEING LAUGHED AT AND ASK

GOD WHAT SHE HAD DONE SO
WRONG SO BAD

NOTHING SHOULD HURT THE
WAY THAT SHE HURT

NO GIRL SHOULD HAVE TO STAY
SO SAD

SO FINALLY SHE WAS ABOUT TO
LOSE HER MIND

NOTHING SEEMS TO EVER GIVE

SHE WAS HURT AND
EMBARRASSED AND ALONE

SHE COULDN'T FIND ANY MORE
REASONS LEFT FOR HER TO LIVE

SHE WENT WITHOUT A WARNING
WITHOUT A SOUND AT ALL

SHE HUNG HERSELF TO PLEASE
THEIR MINDLESS JOKES

BUT IN SHOCK THEY WERE AT
SCHOOL THE NEXT DAY

WHEN THEY DISCOVERED THAT
THE REASON THEY PREVOKED.


## GRINDING

TO HAVE GAINED SO MUCH
WISDOM IN SUCH LITTLE TIME

SOMETIMES MY IGNORANCE
STILL AMAZES ME

I KNOW THE OUTCOME FOR FAR
TOO MANY TIMES OVER AGAIN

YET I GO STUCK ON STUPID AND
THE CONSEQUENCES ARE
MYSTER

SO NOW HERE WE ARE ANOTHER
NIGHT ADDED A LENGTHY LIST

MY BACK ACHES AND MY
WALLETS THIN

AND IM GRINDING MY TEETH
AND CLENCHING MY FISTS

AGGRAVATED AT THE
CIRCUMSTANCES AND
DISAPPOINTED WITH MYSELF

NOW I REMEMBER THIS SO WELL

AND HELLO, HERE IS THE
DISGUST THAT I HAVE IN
EVERYBODY AND EVERYTHING

OH YEA, THIS IS WHY MY LIFE IS
SHOT TO HELL

CLOUDED BY A MIRAGE OF
SATISFACTION ONLY TO BE
REMINDED I AM COMPLETELY
INSANE

NOW ITS FUCKING TOO LATE

THIS CANNOT BE MY FATE

DEVOURED BY MY BIGGEST
DEMON..THE DOPE GAME

I FINALLY HAD A SENSE OF
PEACE AND A FOG WAS LIFTED
FROM MIND AND I COULD SEE IT
ALL REAL CLEAR

BUT IT TAKES ONE LITTLE SLIP
AND IT IS IN YOUR FACE AND IVE
JUST THROUWN TO THE TRASH
SOBRIETY THAT LASTED A YEAR.

I SEE HOW MY LIFE IS A ROLLER
COASTER SO IT SEEMS I ACT
THAT WAY

AND I SEE HOW DOPE INFECTS
MY HEART AND MIND BODY AND
SOU

AND ALL THAT IS GOOD ROTS IN
DECAY

I NEVER ASK FOR THIS DISEASE

I JUST WANTED TO FIT IN AND
NOT BE LEFT BEHIND

AND BAM.....TWENTY YEARS
LATER BROKE BACK, MISSING
TEETH

I CHEW OFF MY NAILS SITTING
HERE ON THE GRIND

IM DUMB AND IGNORANT BUT
YES TO THIS DISEASE

I AM POWERLESS AND I AM
WEAK

AND I HATE THIS FEELING THAT I
FEEL RIGHT NOW

BUT YET ONNN MY PHONE
ANYWAYS

GONNA FIND WHAT I SET OUT TO
SEEK

## USING ME

AFTER NINETEEN YEARS OF
THINKING I WAS USING YOU TO
FEEL NUMB

I REALIZED IT WAS YOU THAT
WAS USING ME AND I FELT SO
DUMB

I COULD MAKE IT I SWORE ID
WENT TO REHAB BEFORE

I COULD DO THIS ON MY OWN

THEN SOMEONE WOULD COME
KNOCKING AT MY DOOR

THE MORE I USED

THE PAIN I STILL HAD

FIVE ATTEMPTS AT ENDING IT

I ADMITTED IT WAS TOO BAD

I CALLED SERENITY EVERY WEEK

I KNEW I WOULD DIE IF HELP I
DID NOT SEEK

ABOUT FIVE WEEKS LATER THEY
CALLED TO CHECK ON ME

I TOLD THEM I NEEDED A BED
FAST I COULD NOT KEEP WAITING
DON'T THEY SEE

THEY PUT ME ON HOLD AND
WHEN SHE RETURNED TO THE
CALL

SHE SAID SOMEONE HAD
CANCELLED BE THERE
TOMORROW

TO MY KNEES I DID FALL

NOW I SIT HERE.. THIRTY DAYS
HAVE PASSED

AND IM WALKING WTH GOD
AGAIN AT LAST

## BYE, DOPE

FOR 19 YEARS I WORSHIPPED
YOU

LETTING YOU WHOOP MY ASS

SO CUNNING YOU LET ME PUT
YOU ON A PEDASTOOL

WITH ME PUTTING GOD AND MY
KIDS OUT LAST

BLASTING MYSELF INTO THE
CLOUDS TO HIDE ALL THE PAIN
THAT I WOULD FEEL

IN RETURN I WAS LEFT COMING
DOWN

SPINNING IN AN EVIL FERRIS
WHEEL

I HATED THE HIGH AND I HATED
THE LOW BUT I NUMBED ALL
EMOTION BEHIND THE METH

IT SEEMED IT WAS ALL I KNEW
TO DO

WHICH NEARLY LEAD ME TO MY
DEATH.

CLEARING MY HEAD AND
POURING OUT TEARS

I WASHED AWAY WITH THE
PRESENCE OF MY PEERS

STEPHANIE SHOWED THAT
RELAPSE WAS NOT DEALING
WITH EMOTIONS WITHIN ME

AND I CAN BE A BEST FRIEND
AND A SOBER MOM

I AN NOW LIVE LIFE FREEE.

THIS BOOK IS DEDICATED TO MY
MOTHER, LILLIE IVANA
FOUNTAIN.

MAY YOU REST IN PEACE MAMA.

(10/26/62-11/27/16)